JUST ONE POT

Lindsey Bareham

Also by Lindsey Bareham:
 In Praise of the Potato
 A Celebration of Soup
 Onions Without Tears
 Supper Won`t Take Long
 The Little Book of Big Soups
 The Big Red Book of Tomatoes
with Simon Hopkinson:
 Roast Chicken and Other Stories
 The Prawn Cocktail Years

First published in Great Britain in 2004 by Cassell Illustrated,
a division of Octopus Publishing Group Limited
2–4 Heron Quays, London E14 4JP

Distributed in the United States of America by
Sterling Publishing Co., Inc.,
387 Park Avenue South, New York, NY 10016-8810

A CIP catalogue record for this book is available from the British Library.

ISBN 1 84403 162 4

Photographs by Neil Barclay
Prop Styling by Fanny Ward
Food Styling by Joy Davies
Design by Shiny Design
Illustrations by Henry John
Jacket design and Art Direction by Jo Knowles
Publishing Manager Anna Cheifetz
Edited by Lesley Malkin

Printed in China

JUST ONE POT

Lindsey Bareham

CASSELL ILLUSTRATED

CONTENTS

Have you ever totted up how much time and energy you waste washing up the sinkful of saucepans which seem to be required for every meal? Well, neither had I until my cooking life was turned upside down for three months while I had my kitchen ripped out and replaced. Cooking on two burners and using a maximum of two pans for each meal had such a useful effect on my cooking and eliminated so much tedious washing up that I decided to turn the recipes into a book. After all, it seemed to me, if a book will help you provide interesting food for yourself, your family and friends without a load of the worst kind of washing up, who could resist? All the recipes here can be cooked in one, occasionally two, pans (and the second is usually just for preparing vegetables). Some dishes, such as the stews and curries, could be cooked in the oven, but an oven is not essential for any recipe. Occasionally dishes are finished under the grill, but it's rare and never essential to the goodness of the dish.

Most recipes are simple, requiring minimal preparation, and all are made with easily attainable, seasonal ingredients. There are no fiddly, restaurant-style dishes, but there are plenty of tricks of the trade that will upgrade your daily meals. This is after-work food, the daily meal that shouldn't be too demanding to make or take too long to cook. Equally, these dishes are never boring: there are big soups, piled with fresh, seasonal vegetables, sometimes with fish or meat, which are interesting and satisfying enough to be a complete meal. There are numerous ways of turning the staples of life, such as pasta, potatoes, rice and dried beans, into meals to remember. Chicken, which is what most of us turn to repeatedly for quick, after-work meals, makes up one of the biggest chapters with dishes as diverse as Scottish Cock-a-leekie, Thai Chicken tom yam and French After-work coq au vin. Seafood, which is often overlooked as a healthy, fast food, is another big section, with favourites from all around the world including Spanish Cod with white beans, After-work bouillabaisse and Prawn laksa with green beans. Pork, bacon and ham is possibly my favourite section, with hearty dishes such as Cocktail sausage and lentil stew and Dublin coddle. Red meats – Lamb and Beef, veal and venison – are the smallest chapters because, like so many people, I eat less red meat than I used to and I'm fussy about its heritage. That's not to say I could ever resist a properly made Irish stew, or less familiar meaty dishes such as Greek lemon lamb with new potatoes, Frito mallorquin (who would have thought liver could taste so good?) and Smoked chili con carne with cherry tomatoes. The

Vegetarian section grew so large that I considered devoting the whole book to one-pan vegetarian dishes; the possibilities, it seems to me, are endless. Malaysian Gado gado and Macaroni cheese with melting tomatoes is the kind of food I'm talking about. Puddings, too, get a major look in. Chocolate rice pudding, Scottish Cranachan, Eton mess and Apple cream with banana passion fruit sauce is my kind of pudding in a bowl.

A word or two about ingredients: **stock** is key to many of these one-pot dishes. While home-made is always desirable, shop-bought stock is fine for convenience – quick-dissolving granules, cubes or even a can of consommé will all do the trick. I peel stringy **vegetables** like celery with a potato peeler, but potatoes I usually cook first, as the skins are then so much easier to remove. When making a **garlic** paste, check cloves for the little green growing stem, and remove it first – but don't bother if you are chopping or slicing it. Always choose unwaxed **lemons** if the zest is to be used in a recipe.

My time of self-inflicted kitchen denial also proved that you need very little equipment to cook well with comfort and efficiency. I limited myself to a couple of sharp knives and a knife sharpener to keep them perfect; a chopping board; a few wooden spoons; a whisk; a frying pan and a wok; a large heavy-bottomed saucepan and a small one for milk and eggs; a kettle and a toaster. I also relied on a good, swivel-head potato peeler, a colander and a sieve, and my trusty Magimix food processor.

The book reflects the pleasure I found in the challenge of cooking on two burners, but translates perfectly to all of us, all the time. These dishes prove, simply and tastefully, that cooking in one pan makes a lot of sense.

Lindsey Bareham

Vegetarian

It's interesting how the meat-and-two-veg-loving majority has achieved a total volte-face when it comes to vegetarianism. Less than twenty years ago, if you didn't eat meat you were a bit of a weirdo. Yet look at any fashionable menu now, peppered as it is with dish after dish without meat or fish, or check out the chill counter of any supermarket, and you'll find the choice on offer is extraordinarily diverse. Vegetarian cooking has become a favourite with adventurous cooks, and meals can be a feast for all the senses – a mixture of colours, flavours and textures. Although I am never likely to give up meat and fish completely, I'm typical of the new breed of quasi-vegetarians who no longer think that meat is essential in a balanced diet. My cooking has changed over recent years towards vegetarianism – prompted as much by food scares as the high price of properly reared meat. Without making a conscious effort, I eat meat-and-fish-free meals at least three times a week, sometimes more often.

Even so, it was quite a shock when I annotated my recipes for inclusion in this book to discover that this section was the largest and most difficult to prune down. Onion and rosemary risotto with Marsala, Autumn vegetable ragout and Italian rocket and potato soup is the sort of food I'm talking about, as is Potato salad with watercress. These dishes are delicious in their own right, and are satisfying enough, in terms of texture and colour as well as flavour, that no one notices the lack of meat. It is the sort of food that keeps us in touch with the seasons. Vegetables are also comparatively simple and inexpensive to shop for; in many places now it is increasingly easy to buy organic vegetables from farmers' markets, regional suppliers and the supermarkets.

I've found that the more I turn towards a vegetarian diet, the more conscious I am of the effect that certain foods have on my metabolism and general well being. Information on how food affects us, in terms of mood as well as nutrition, is widely available from many sources and is both interesting and useful to know. Lentils, for example, man's oldest food, are good for reducing cholesterol, stress and nervous exhaustion, while nature's other comfort food and one of my favourites, the wonderfully versatile potato, is packed with minerals and vitamins.

Asparagus risotto

Serves 4   *10 minutes preparation: 30 minutes cooking*

The useful thing about this risotto is that it doesn't rely on being made with a special stock. Instead, the asparagus cooking liquid is bolstered with stock granules. The cooked stalks, as opposed to the tips, are chopped and liquidized with a little of the asparagus stock, and this bright green sauce is stirred into the risotto along with the tender tips, at the end of cooking. The risotto is finished with what seems like a huge amount of grated Parmesan and a knob of butter.

500g/1lb asparagus
50g/2oz butter
squeeze lemon
1 heaped tsp vegetable stock granules
1 small onion or shallot

200g/7oz arborio rice
½ wine glass Noilly Prat, vermouth or white wine
4 heaped tbsp freshly grated Parmesan cheese plus
  extra to serve
salt and freshly ground black pepper

Trim and discard the woody ends of the asparagus. Cut off the tender tips and set aside. Cut the remaining stalks into chunks. In a suitable saucepan, bring 900ml/1½ pints water to the boil. Add a generous pinch of salt and the asparagus tips. Bring the water back to the boil and cook for 2 minutes. Scoop the tips out of the water and drain. Drop the stalks into the water and cook for 4 minutes or until completely tender. Reduce the heat and scoop out of the pan.

Place the stalks and a cup of the cooking water into the bowl of a food processor with a knob of butter. Blitz to make a smooth purée. If necessary, pass the purée through a sieve. Taste and adjust the flavour with salt, pepper and a squeeze of lemon. Dissolve the stock granules in the rest of the cooking water, then pour into a jug or bowl and cover to keep hot.

Peel and finely chop the onion or shallot. Melt half of the remaining butter in a heavy saucepan and gently cook the onion until soft but not coloured – about 3 minutes. Add the rice and cook with the onion until the rice is glistening and semi-translucent – about 2 minutes. As soon as the rice turns shiny and even more translucent, add the Noilly Prat. It will seethe and then bubble away into the rice, but make sure you stir as it does so. Add a ladleful of the hot stock. Stir as it sizzles and then cook for a couple of minutes, stirring constantly, until the rice has absorbed most of the liquid. Add a second ladleful of stock and stir until all the liquid is absorbed, adjusting the heat to maintain a gentle simmer.

Continue in this way, stirring constantly, until the rice is almost tender but firm to the bite, about 20–30 minutes in total. The risotto should have a creamy, porridge-like consistency. Remove from the heat. Stir in the asparagus purée, the asparagus tips, the remaining butter and the cheese. Cover and leave for 5 minutes to finish cooking. Serve sprinkled with the extra Parmesan.

Cherry tomato gazpacho

Serves 6–8   *25 minutes preparation*

The great thing about using cherry tomatoes for Spanish gazpacho, as opposed to regular tomatoes, is that their flavour is reliably intense. Gazpacho is the perfect thing to eat on a hot day. It's often described as the salad soup because it's made with ingredients that would make a fine salad. When served with its full complement of garnishes, as here, it becomes a meal in itself.

4 thick slices white bread, without crusts, about
   150g/5oz
2 plump garlic cloves, peeled
1 cucumber
1 red chilli
2 red peppers, preferably 'extra sweet' pointed type
1 red onion
1kg/2lb cherry tomatoes or ripe vine tomatoes

2 tbsp sherry vinegar or wine vinegar
300ml/½ pint cold water
about 20 mint leaves
100ml/3½fl oz olive oil plus 2 tbsp
3 plum or vine tomatoes
squeeze lemon juice
Tabasco sauce
salt and freshly ground black pepper

Tear the bread into pieces. Place it and the peeled garlic in the bowl of a food processor and blitz to make fine breadcrumbs.

Peel the cucumber. Halve it lengthways and use a teaspoon to scrape out the seeds. Chop half roughly. Trim and split the chilli and scrape out the seeds. Set aside half of one red pepper and chop the rest, discarding seeds and white membrane. Peel and halve the onion. Coarsely chop one half and add to the breadcrumbs in the food processor bowl together with the chopped cucumber, chilli and chopped red pepper.

Remove the stalks from the cherry or vine tomatoes and add them to the food processor bowl with the vinegar, water, most of the mint, the 100ml/3½fl oz olive oil, ½ teaspoon of salt and a generous seasoning of black pepper. Blitz for several minutes until liquidized.

Meanwhile, prepare the garnishes. Keeping separate piles, finely dice the remaining cucumber and red pepper and finely chop the remaining red onion. Quarter the plum or vine tomatoes, discard the seeds and chop finely. Taste the gazpacho and adjust the seasoning with salt, pepper, lemon juice and Tabasco. Transfer to a chilled serving bowl and decorate with a swirl of olive oil. Serve with the garnishes in small bowls, adding the remaining mint leaves to the tomato.

Autumn vegetable ragout

Serves 4–6   *20 minutes preparation: 30 minutes cooking*

Cold, damp weather is comfort-food time. A steaming bowl of chunky vegetables is the culinary equivalent of a nice warm hug. I hesitate to call this a big bowlful of soup because the proportion of vegetables to liquid makes it more like a stew. The trick here is to cook the vegetables in the right order for the right length of time so that the background stuff, like potatoes and onions, is soft and tender and the green vegetables keep a bit of bite. Chilli and garlic are added at the beginning to lend soul rather than fire. If you feel inclined, cover each bowl with grated Cheddar or Parmesan and add a dollop of pesto. I like to dip big slabs of garlic-rubbed toast into the soup.

1 onion
2 large garlic cloves
1 red chilli
3 tbsp olive oil
4 potatoes
1 large carrot
1 red pepper

1 leek
1 vegetable stock cube dissolved in 1 litre/1¾ pints
   boiling water
450g/14½oz broccoli florets
handful of mangetout or sugar snap peas
salt and freshly ground black pepper
lemon wedges to serve

Peel, halve and finely chop the onion and garlic. Trim and split the chilli, wipe away the seeds and finely chop. Don't forget to wash your hands now with soapy water to get rid of the lethal chilli juices that will burn sensitive parts.

Gently soften the onion, garlic and chilli in the olive oil in a decent-sized, heavy-based saucepan placed over a medium-low heat. Stir every so often while you get chopping. Peel the potatoes, chop into kebab-sized chunks and rinse. Peel the carrots and chop slightly smaller. Stir the potatoes and carrots into the softened and lightly browned onions and season generously with salt and black pepper. Cover and cook, stirring once or twice, for 5 minutes.

Meanwhile, finely chop the red pepper, discarding seeds and white membrane, and thickly slice the white part of the leek; keep the greens for later. Stir the red pepper and leek white into the pan, cover again and leave for a few more minutes before adding the stock. Return the pan to the boil, reduce the heat slightly and cook, uncovered, for 5–6 minutes, or until the potatoes are just tender.

Cut the broccoli into bite-sized florets and slice down the mangetout or sugar snaps to make 3 or 4 strips. Finely slice the leek greens and wash thoroughly. Add all three to the pot, taste the broth and adjust the seasoning. Boil steadily for 2–3 minutes, or until you are satisfied that the broccoli is *al dente*. Serve immediately with a wedge of lemon to squeeze over the top.

Fattoush

Serves 4–6   *30 minutes preparation: 2 minutes cooking*

Fattoush is a Middle Eastern salad which pops up on many Lebanese menus. To be really authentic you will need to hunt out a blend of Middle Eastern herbs called za'atar which includes a tart, red spice called sumac. This is the red dust that decorates and seasons much Middle Eastern food, and is often sprinkled over onion salads. I'm not convinced that any of these extra sharp, resinous flavours are essential to the success of the already acidic and nutty salad. To get maximum pleasure from making this salad, you will need two sharp knives: one small triangular turning or paring knife and a larger broad-pointed cook's knife. This is most definitely a salad that is all about chopping and slicing and it will be misery to attempt with a blunt knife.

1 cucumber
4 large shallots or 100g/3½ oz bunch spring
   onions or 2 medium red onions
500g/1lb tomatoes
1 celery heart or 4 peeled sticks
1 slice pitta bread
1 large bunch flat leaf parsley, at least 80g/3oz

2 plump garlic cloves
juice 1 lemon
6 tbsp olive oil
1 tbsp roughly chopped mint
3 tbsp roughly chopped coriander
salt and freshly ground black pepper

Use a potato peeler to peel the cucumber, split lengthways and use a teaspoon to gouge out the seeds. Cut into lengths and dice the flesh. Tip into a colander, dredge with 1 tablespoon salt and leave to drain while you do all the rest of the chopping.

Peel and finely dice the shallots, spring onions or onions. Place the tomatoes in a bowl, cover with boiling water, count to 20 and drain. Quarter the tomatoes and flake away the skin. Use your fingers or a teaspoon to remove the seeds. Dice the flesh. Trim, then very finely slice the celery, tip into a colander and rinse thoroughly under cold running water. Drain carefully.

Split the pitta bread in half and toast both sides until crisp. When cool enough to handle, crumble up the bread into small pieces. Pick all the leaves off the parsley stalks and chop very finely. Peel the garlic, chop roughly, then sprinkle with a scant ½ teaspoon of salt and pulverize with the flat of a blade to make a creamy paste. Tip the garlic paste into a salad bowl, stir in the lemon juice and whisk in the olive oil. Tip in the onions, then the celery, and finally the tomatoes and herbs, stirring as you make each addition.

Rinse the salt from the cucumber, drain thoroughly and pat dry with kitchen paper. Add to the salad and season generously with black pepper. Give one final toss and strew the pitta bread crumbs over the top. Five minutes before you are ready to eat, fold in the crumbs.

Eggs masala

Serves 4   *15 minutes preparation: 40 minutes cooking*

If you have a can of tomatoes in the cupboard, you are never very far from a delicious supper. If you also have a couple of onions, some eggs and a decent collection of Indian spices, you can knock up this lovely curry supper. There is something immensely pleasing about the texture and mild flavour of hard-boiled eggs with a thick and chunky tomato and onion curry spiked at the last moment with a handful of fresh coriander. It is delicious with warmed Indian bread to scoop and mop, but becomes more of a meal with rice, poppadoms and your favourite pickles.

4 garlic cloves
2.5cm/1in piece fresh ginger
2 cardamom pods
1 tsp coriander seeds
1 tsp cumin seeds
½ tsp whole cloves
½ tsp black peppercorns
½ tsp cayenne pepper

500g/1lb ripe tomatoes or 400g/14oz can
　chopped tomatoes
6–8 eggs, hard-boiled
2 large onions
2 tbsp vegetable oil
lemon juice
2 tbsp fresh coriander leaves
salt

Peel and chop the garlic. Peel and grate the ginger. Remove the seeds from the cardamom pods. Grind the cardamom, coriander seeds, cumin, cloves and black peppercorns to a powder in a food processor or coffee grinder and then add the garlic, ginger and 2 tablespoons of water. Blitz to make a stiff masala paste and stir in the cayenne pepper.

If using ripe tomatoes, pour boiling water over them, count to 20 and drain. Remove the core and peel, then roughly chop. Peel the hard-boiled eggs and halve lengthways.

Meanwhile, peel and finely dice the onions. Heat the oil in a wok or large saucepan over a medium-high heat and fry the onions until they turn caramel brown, stirring constantly so they brown evenly. Allow at least 20 minutes. Stir the masala paste into the onions and stir-fry for a couple of minutes. Add the tomatoes and a generous pinch of salt. Simmer vigorously for 10–15 minutes until the sauce begins to thicken. Taste and adjust the seasoning with more salt and lemon juice. If the tomatoes weren't ripe enough, you may need to add a little sugar and a slug of ketchup.

Get the sauce very hot, stir in most of the fresh coriander and place the eggs, sunny-side up, in the sauce. Continue simmering until the eggs are warmed through. Sprinkle on the last of the fresh coriander and serve with basmati rice, raita and mango chutney.

Fragrant mushroom curry with green beans

Serves 4   *15 minutes preparation: 35 minutes cooking*

This isn't an overly hot curry, more of a fragrant gravy with a gentle back heat, but a sensible and delicious accompaniment would be a bowl of raita or thick natural yoghurt stirred with grated cucumber. I like to serve it with basmati rice or warm nan bread or chapatis to scoop up the copious and delicious juices. If you eat seafood, a good addition to this curry, in terms of flavour, texture and colour, is a handful of cooked prawns, added just before the garam masala.

1 large onion
2 tbsp cooking oil
1 plump red chilli, about 7cm x 3cm/3in x 1½in
200g/7oz green beans
2 rounded tsp curry powder
200ml/7fl oz carton coconut cream
½ chicken stock cube dissolved in 250ml/8fl oz
  boiling water

500g/1lb button mushrooms or quartered medium
  mushrooms
2 medium tomatoes
squeeze lemon juice
1 rounded tsp garam masala
handful coriander leaves
salt and freshly ground black pepper

Peel, halve and finely chop the onion. Add the oil and then the onion to a spacious, heavy-based saucepan placed over a medium-low heat. Cook, stirring often, for 10–15 minutes until the onion is soft but uncoloured. Meanwhile, trim and split the chilli and scrape away the seeds. Chop into tiny dice. Stir the chilli into the onions and cook for a couple of minutes while you top and tail the beans (I never remove the pointed ends) and cut them in half.

Stir the curry powder into the onions and cook, stirring constantly, for 2 more minutes. Add the beans to the pan, increase the heat slightly and cook, stirring every so often, for 3 minutes. Add the coconut cream and the stock, give the dish a good stir and leave to simmer for a couple of minutes. Wipe the mushrooms and add them to the pan. Cook, stirring often, for about 8 minutes until cooked through.

Chop the tomatoes (I would peel and seed them, but skin and seed don't spoil the dish) and stir them into the curry. Cook for a few more minutes until warmed through. Now taste the gravy and adjust the seasoning with salt, pepper and lemon juice. Sprinkle over the garam masala, cook for a further minute before serving strewn with coriander leaves.

Gado gado

Serves 4   *25 minutes preparation: 15 minutes cooking*

Gado gado is excellent fridge-tidying food. It's an Indonesian vegetable salad dressed with a spicy peanut sauce and almost anything goes. What you're aiming at is a good mixture of crisp, crunchy textures, so bean sprouts, green beans, cucumber and carrot are de rigueur. *Hard-boiled egg is always present and the warm salad is often turned into more of a meal by the addition of fried tofu. The satay-style, spicy peanut sauce saves the salad from blandness. In restaurants, gado gado is arranged in layers on a large platter as part of a spread. When serving it as family fare, it is wiser to make four separate plates.*

300g/10oz block tofu/beancurd
1 large carrot
½ small white cabbage
150g/5oz green beans
100g/3½oz young spinach leaves
2 Little Gem lettuce hearts
1 small cucumber
2 potatoes, boiled and peeled
4 shallots or 2 small red onions

200g/7oz cauliflower or broccoli florets
100g/3½oz bean sprouts
3 tbsp vegetable oil
2 tbsp flour
2 eggs, hard-boiled
4 tbsp satay peanut sauce or 3 tbsp peanut butter
  thinned with lime or lemon juice, water and
  Tabasco
salt

Place the tofu on a plate and weight with a second plate to draw out the liquid. Meanwhile, put a large saucepan of water on to boil. Keeping separate piles, prepare the vegetables. Peel the carrot and slice into matchsticks. Halve the cabbage, cut out the core and slice thinly across the wedge. Trim the green beans and cut in half. Shred the spinach. Finely shred the lettuce, wash and dry. Peel the cucumber and slice finely. Chop the potatoes. Peel, halve and finely slice the shallots or onions.

Generously salt the boiling water. Add the carrots, bring back to the boil and boil for 1 minute. Scoop into a colander. Repeat with the cabbage, beans and cauliflower or broccoli. Transfer the drained vegetables to a large mixing bowl. Now place the bean sprouts in the colander, pour over the cooking water and shake to drain. Add bean sprouts, spinach, lettuce and cucumber to the bowl and lightly toss everything together.

Arrange the salad in a pyramid on four dinner plates. Scatter the chopped potatoes on top. Heat the oil in the saucepan while you pat dry the tofu and cut it into strips. Toss the strips in the flour and fry quickly in hot oil until lightly golden. Remove from the pan to drain and add the shallots to the pan. Fry quickly until crisp and golden. Drain. Add the tofu to the salad, decorate with wedges of hard-boiled egg, pour over the peanut sauce and sprinkle with the fried shallots.

Goanese potato curry

Serves 2–4   *30 minutes preparation: 30 minutes cooking*

This wonderful potato curry is rich and interesting enough to serve on its own. It is good, too, with quartered, hard-boiled eggs and a handful of boiled green beans stirred into the curry at the last moment. I like it scooped up in hot Indian bread with raita and mango chutney. If you need a serious carbohydrate fix, and I admit this is one of my favourite night-after-the-night-before meals, serve it with rice and dal. Coconut cream, incidentally, is pressed and processed fresh coconut and is sold in convenient 200ml/7fl oz cartons. I always keep one or two in the store cupboard because I prefer its thick creaminess to canned coconut. You can use canned or creamed coconut – the one that looks like a slab of lard – instead, made up to packet instructions.

750g/1½lb Jersey Royal or other new potatoes
2 onions
2 tbsp vegetable oil
1 small red or green chilli
3 garlic cloves
3 tsp ground cinnamon
2 tsp coriander seeds or 3 tsp ground coriander

200ml/7fl oz coconut cream
500g/1lb tomatoes
100g/3½oz frozen petits pois
1 lime
handful coriander leaves
salt and freshly ground black pepper

Peel and rinse the potatoes, then boil them in plenty of salted water until tender to the point of a knife. Drain and leave to cool. Meanwhile, peel, halve and thinly slice the onions. Heat the oil in a spacious frying pan or similarly wide-based saucepan until very hot. Stir in the onions and let them brown lightly. Reduce the heat and cook, stirring occasionally, for about 10 minutes until limp and soft.

Meanwhile, trim and split the chilli and scrape away the seeds. Chop. Peel and chop the garlic. Stir the chilli, garlic, cinnamon and coriander seeds or ground coriander into the onions and cook for a couple of minutes before adding the coconut cream. Simmer gently for 5 minutes, then remove and liquidize the mixture to make a thick, creamy, speckled beige sauce. Return the sauce to the pan.

Pour boiling water over the tomatoes, count to 20, drain and peel. Chop the tomatoes and place in a saucepan with 250ml/8fl oz water. Boil for about 10 minutes, then sieve the tomatoes directly into the sauce, pressing hard to extract maximum pulp. Cut the potatoes into bite-sized chunks and add them too. Finally, cook the petits pois in boiling salted water and add them to the dish. Season generously with salt and lightly with pepper. Cook for a few minutes, then squeeze over the lime juice. Taste and adjust the seasoning. Garnish with coriander leaves and serve. Excellent hot, warm or cold.

Italian rocket and potato soup

Serves 2 *15 minutes preparation: 30 minutes cooking*

It's hard to believe that such an ordinary collection of ingredients makes such a delicious soup. I came across zuppa dei poveri con la rucola *years ago when I was doing research for a book. It's been a regular treat ever since and is often something I make when I have a few leftover boiled potatoes in need of using up. It's known as poor man's soup because potatoes, bread and rocket, which grows like a weed in Italy and anywhere it gets a chance to establish itself, are regarded as peasant food. My version ends up thick and rustic and the flavours are enriched with stock, garlic and olive oil. A sprig of rosemary scents the soup with its wild woodland flavours and the last-minute garnish of a splash of extra virgin olive oil enriches and unifies all the ingredients.*

250g/8oz salad or other waxy potatoes	1 sprig rosemary
1 vegetable stock cube	50g/2oz stale or unbaked ciabatta bread
1 onion	100g/3½oz rocket
1 plump garlic clove	3 tbsp extra virgin olive oil
1 tbsp olive oil	salt and freshly ground black pepper

Boil the unpeeled potatoes in plenty of salted water until tender. Drain, measuring off 750ml/1¼ pints of the cooking water, return the potatoes to the pan and cover with cold water. Leave for a couple of minutes, drain again and remove the skins. Cut into chunks.

Dissolve the stock cube in the reserved potato water. Meanwhile, peel, halve and chop the onion and garlic. Heat the tablespoon of oil in a heavy-based saucepan and stir in the onion, garlic and rosemary. Cook, stirring often, for about 8 minutes until the onions are soft but not crisp. Meanwhile, chop the bread into bite-sized chunks.

Stir in the potatoes, add the stock, season with salt and pepper and bring the liquid to the boil. Stir in the rocket, reduce the heat and, as soon as it is wilted, add the bread, stirring it as it drinks up the soup and softens. Dribble over the extra virgin olive oil, remove from the heat, cover and leave for a few minutes before serving with a final twist of pepper.

Greek potato salad with coriander

Serves 4   *15 minutes preparation: 15 minutes cooking*

I could never give up potatoes for very long. I love them so much that I wrote a book, In Praise of the Potato, *devoted to them. I adapted this recipe from the chapter on potato salads and it goes with everything from a slab of feta and a hard-boiled egg, to fish, chicken or lamb. This latest version ups the quantity of coriander and specifies red rather than any other onion. The result is a very pretty salad streaked with red and thick with green leaves. It is the perfect thing for a barbecue when you might echo the Greek theme with hummus, taramasalata, stuffed vine leaves, a Greek salad and lamb kebabs. Stuff the lot into warmed split Greek bread. Yum.*

750g/1½lb similar-sized new potatoes
1 red onion
2 garlic cloves
65g/2½oz bunch coriander

2 tbsp wine vinegar
4 tbsp good quality extra virgin olive oil
salt and freshly ground black pepper

Scrub or peel the potatoes, rinse and cook in plenty of salted boiling water until tender. Drain. Leave small potatoes whole, halve medium potatoes and cut large ones into chunks.

Meanwhile, peel, halve and finely slice the onion. Peel and chop the garlic. Trim the coarse stalk ends of the bunch of coriander. Keeping the bunch shape, finely chop the stalks and let the chopping get progressively coarser as you work up the bunch into the leaves.

Pour the vinegar into a salad bowl and add a generous pinch of salt and several grinds of black pepper. Swirl the vinegar around the bowl until the salt has dissolved. Whisk in the olive oil to make a thick and luscious dressing. Stir in the garlic and onion and then add the hot potatoes. Stir thoroughly and add the chopped coriander. Stir again and serve hot, warm or cold, giving a final stir just before serving.

Macaroni cheese with melting tomatoes

Serves 4   *15 minutes preparation: 15 minutes cooking*

When I think of macaroni cheese – and Monday night, with its combination of empty food cupboards, minimal interest in shopping and cooking, and the need for something comforting to eat is when it usually happens – I imagine it with a crusty, cheesy topping. This equally delicious version is risotto-style: sloppy and gorgeous. Non-vegetarians may choose to add crunch from crisp nuggets of fried smoked pancetta or bacon, added straight after the macaroni.

4 tomatoes, halved
1 tbsp olive oil
200g/7oz macaroni
100g/3½oz bunch spring onions
25g/1oz butter
25g/1oz flour

½ tbsp smooth Dijon mustard
300ml/½ pint milk
150g/5oz hard cheese, grated, plus extra to serve
chives to serve
salt and freshly ground black pepper

First cook the tomatoes. This can be done under the grill, in the oven, in a frying pan, or in the pasta pan before the pasta. If grilling or cooking in the oven, smear the cut surfaces with olive oil; if frying, add the oil to the pan and cook gently until completely soft. Allow at least 10 minutes for this. Next, cook the macaroni in plenty of salted boiling water according to the packet instructions. Drain and cover to keep warm.

Meanwhile, trim and finely slice the spring onions. Add the butter to the saucepan, stir in the onions and cook for a couple of minutes until softened. Stir in the flour, continuing until it disappears. Add the mustard and gradually incorporate the milk, beating briskly as it begins to boil to make a smooth sauce. Reduce the heat and cook gently for about 5 minutes to cook the flour. Stir in the cheese. Taste and adjust the seasoning with salt and pepper.

Stir the macaroni into the sauce. Serve risotto-style with a garnish of grated cheese and chopped chives and the tomatoes on the side.

Moroccan salad

Serves 2   *15 minutes preparation: 15 minutes cooking*

I once stayed at the most amazing 'hotel' just outside Marrakech where guests came together in a candlelit garden restaurant. The meal began with the ubiquitous Moroccan salad, a dish that features all over Morocco and is never the same twice, even at the same restaurant. This time it was served mezze-style in a series of dishes. Green lentils came with slivers of red onion; grated carrot and courgettes were seasoned with fresh coriander and cumin; and crescents of cucumber had been pickled and sweetened with sugar and served icy cold. Another dish contained peeled and semi-carved radishes, another a sweet tomato jam that was so thick it could be carved into ridges. This stupendous feast was served with a wheel of flat bread decorated with different seeds and was virtually a meal in itself. My ersatz version makes a satisfying, healthy supper with toasted pitta or another flat bread such as focaccia and crisp lettuce leaves to scoop it up.

12 small scrubbed new potatoes	1 carrot
4 tomatoes	1 small red onion
1 tsp ground cumin	400g/14oz can green lentils
1 tsp runny honey	1 small lemon
4 tbsp olive oil	2 tbsp chopped coriander
150g/5oz green beans	salt and freshly ground black pepper

Cook the potatoes in salted boiling water until tender. Drain and leave to cool. Halve the tomatoes, slicing round tomatoes through their plump middles and plum tomatoes lengthways. Season each half with a pinch of cumin, salt and pepper. Dribble with a little honey and olive oil. Pre-heat the grill to medium. Arrange the tomato halves on the grill pan and cook, checking so they don't burn, for about 10 minutes until very soft.

Meanwhile, put a pan of water on for the beans. Trim the beans (I don't bother to remove the pointy ends) and cut in half. Cook the beans in boiling water for 2 minutes. Drain. Trim and peel the carrot. Grate it through a small hole on the cheese grater or appropriate attachment of a food processor.

Peel and halve the onion and slice wafer-thin. Tip the lentils into a sieve and rinse under cold water. Shake dry. Squeeze the lemon juice into a salad bowl. Add the rest of the cumin and a pinch of salt and pepper and whisk in the remaining olive oil. Stir in the onion, then add the potatoes, beans, carrot, lentils and coriander. Toss well and arrange the tomatoes over the top.

Onion and rosemary risotto with Marsala

Serves 2   *15 minutes preparation: 30 minutes cooking*

This is a terrific store-cupboard risotto to warm up a chilly autumn night. It demands few fresh ingredients, but the combination of onion, rosemary and Marsala creates a deliciously rich flavour. The rice should be soft and creamy on the outside with a slight bite on the inside. If it isn't, just add a little more hot water and continue simmering for a few more minutes.

2 medium-sized onions and 1 small onion
1 heaped tsp rosemary leaves
1 tbsp vegetable oil
75g/3oz butter
250g/8oz arborio rice
1 small glass Marsala

approximately 1 litre/1¾ pints hot vegetable stock
   (fresh is best but cube is fine)
50g/2oz Parmesan cheese, grated, plus extra
   to serve
pinch sugar
salt and freshly ground black pepper

Peel, halve and thinly slice all 3 onions, keeping the small slices in a pile on their own. Very finely chop the rosemary leaves to resemble green dust. Fry the small onion in hot vegetable oil in a medium-sized heavy-based saucepan (large enough to hold the entire dish), tossing it around until crisp. Drain on absorbent kitchen paper. Melt 50g/2oz of the butter in the pan over a medium heat. Stir in the large sliced onions, season with ½ teaspoon salt, cover the pan and cook for about 15 minutes until limp.

Stir the rosemary into the limp onions. Add the rice and cook with the onion for a couple of minutes until the rice is glistening and semi-translucent. As soon as the rice turns shiny and even more translucent, add the Marsala. It will seethe, then bubble away into the rice, but make sure you stir as it does so. Add a ladleful of hot stock. Stir as it sizzles, stirring constantly and cooking for a couple of minutes until the rice has absorbed most of the liquid. Add a second ladleful of stock and stir until all the liquid is absorbed, adjusting the heat to maintain a gentle simmer. Continue in this way, stirring constantly, until the rice is almost tender but firm to the bite – between 20 and 30 minutes in total, until the risotto has a creamy, porridge-like consistency.

Remove the pan from the heat. Stir in the remaining butter and the cheese. Cover the pan and leave for 5 minutes before adjusting the seasoning with salt, pepper and a little sugar. Serve with a garnish of the crisply fried onions and extra Parmesan.

One-eyed bouillabaisse with peas

Serves 2 *20 minutes preparation: 15 minutes cooking*

Most people know bouillabaisse, the Mediterranean fishermen's soup. The one-eyed version – made with vegetables and eggs – is far less exacting than the original, but is nonetheless a wonderful dish and something to make in the summer when fresh peas and slim leeks are available. This bouillabaisse is more rustic than the famous fish soup, but the principles are identical. Bouillabaisse is named after a method of cooking – bouillon-abaisse – meaning broth rapidly boiled to reduce. More olive oil than you would have thought necessary goes into it, but part of the point of the boiling process is to homogenize the oil with the cooking water. This results in a rich and surprisingly tasty broth also flavoured by garlic, orange zest, a bay leaf and a few sprigs of thyme, and rosemary too. A generous pinch of saffron stamens is the only luxury ingredient, and in this bouillabaisse it haunts rather than dominates the flavouring, as is often the case in the fish versions dished up in the Mediterranean.

1 leek	1 bay leaf
1 shallot or small red onion	2 strips paper-thin orange zest
3 large garlic cloves	pinch saffron stamens, dissolved in 1 tbsp
2 large tomatoes	boiling water
1 small courgette	200g/7oz peas (shelled weight) or frozen petits pois
6 new potatoes	2 eggs
5 tbsp olive oil	2 thick slices country-style bread
3 sprigs thyme	1 tbsp finely chopped flat leaf parsley
1 small sprig rosemary	salt and freshly ground black pepper

Trim the leek, slice in 1cm/½in rounds, rinse and drain. Peel the shallot or onion and chop. Peel the garlic, slice two of the cloves thinly and cut the third in half. Cover the tomatoes with boiling water, count to 20, drain, core and peel. Remove the seeds and chop the flesh.

Chop the courgette into small pieces, discarding the ends. Peel the potatoes, slice into thick discs, rinse and shake dry. Place 4 tablespoons of the olive oil into a large saucepan over a medium heat and briefly fry the leek and shallot or onion with the sliced garlic, thyme, rosemary, bay leaf and orange zest. Add the saffron, 600ml/1 pint boiling water, the potatoes and the tomatoes, and season generously with salt and pepper. Increase the heat to the highest possible setting and boil for 5–6 minutes, or until the potatoes are tender. Add the peas and courgette and cook until tender. Taste and adjust the seasoning.

When the soup is ready, reduce the heat and crack the eggs into it. Simmer gently until the eggs are set. Meanwhile, toast the bread and rub with the cut garlic. Place the toast in two soup bowls and dribble with the remaining olive oil. Using a slotted spoon, lift the egg onto the toast, spoon vegetables around it and pour on the broth. Sprinkle with parsley and eat.

Potato salad with watercress

Serves 2–4   *20 minutes preparation: 15 minutes cooking*

You can't go wrong with potato salad. Not, that is, if you make it yourself and use decent ingredients for the dressing. This one was inspired by a recipe of French chef Joel Robuchon. My version of this great chef's watercress potato salad is more homespun than the original, but is none the worse for that. Two of us shared the salad and nothing but a smear of dressing was left in the bowl although M. Robuchon suggests that the dish will feed four to six people. It went down very nicely with slices of Parma ham, farmhouse Cheddar and crusty bread and butter.

**500g/1lb new potatoes such as Jersey Royal or
  a waxy or salad variety such as Charlotte
2 eggs, hard-boiled
1 shallot
2 scant tbsp white wine vinegar
6 scant tbsp olive oil**

**3 tbsp finely chopped flat leaf parsley
2 tbsp finely sliced chives
1 tbsp finely chopped mint
50g/2oz trimmed and washed watercress
salt and freshly ground black pepper**

Scrape Jersey Royals (or other new potatoes with flaky skins) but leave smooth-skinned varieties with skins intact. Boil in plenty of salted water until tender to the point of a knife. Drain. Return smooth-skinned varieties to cold water and leave for a minute before removing the skins. Peel the eggs, preferably while still hot.

While the potatoes cook, peel, halve and finely chop the shallot. Place the vinegar in a salad bowl, season with salt and pepper and, when the salt has dissolved, whisk in the oil to make a thick emulsion. Stir the shallot into the vinaigrette. Slice the hot potatoes directly into the dressing and stir well. Leave for a few minutes for the dressing to soak into and flavour the potatoes, then grate the eggs directly over the top. The dish looks prettiest if you force the eggs through a small hole on the grater, but you will have to scratch out the clogged holes.

Season with black pepper and a little salt and pile on the chopped herbs. Gently stir everything together. Now pile the watercress on top. Serve immediately while the potatoes are still warm but not hot enough to wilt the watercress.

Salsa cruda tortilla pizza

Serves 2–4   *10 minutes preparation: 5 minutes cooking*

Soft flour tortillas, the sort used in numerous ways in countless Mexican dishes and more recently as sandwich wraps, make a brilliant standby for quick, interesting suppers. Given a quick blast of heat to make them puff and crisp, they make surprisingly good, lightweight pizza bases for almost any food and don't require cooking. Try button mushrooms fried with garlic and parsley, stirred into a spicy tomato sauce, for example. This 'pizza' is spread with pesto, then generously piled with a colourful, chunky salsa-cum-salad which looks as good as it tastes. A generous crumble of feta or goat's cheese makes the pizza amazingly satisfying. I'd say you need two each for supper, but one makes a great starter.

400g/14oz cherry tomatoes
10 cornichons or 1 small pickled cucumber
15 good-quality black olives
about 15 basil leaves
200g/7oz feta or semi-hard goat's cheese
4 tbsp pesto

1 tbsp lemon juice
1 tbsp olive oil
1 tbsp vegetable oil
4 flour tortillas
sea salt and freshly ground black pepper

Chop the cherry tomatoes then scoop the pieces onto a big plate or into a mixing bowl. Quarter the cornichons or pickled cucumber lengthways and then slice across into little chunks. Slice the flesh off the olives in 3 or 4 pieces. Add the cornichons or pickled cucumber and olives to the tomatoes. Season lightly with salt and generously with black pepper.

Shred the basil over the salad and crumble the feta on top. If using a firmer goat's cheese, chop it finely. Loosely mix the ingredients. Spoon 1 tablespoon of the pesto into a small bowl and stir in the lemon juice and olive oil. Heat a frying pan with a quarter of the vegetable oil or an un-oiled griddle for a couple of minutes until very hot. If using a griddle, lightly smear both sides of the tortilla with oil. Lay out a tortilla, pressing it down with a fish slice for a few seconds, as it immediately begins to puff and brown underneath. Turn and cook the other side. Repeat to cook the remaining tortilla.

Spread the tortilla with the undiluted pesto, then pile the salsa cruda on top. Give the pesto dressing a final stir and dribble it over the top of the pizzas. Serve immediately.

Spaghetti with garlic, chilli and herbs

Serves 2   *15 minutes preparation: 15 minutes cooking*

This is an incredibly quick, simple and delicious pasta dish. Apart from the herbs, which are an optional add-on to a classic combination, this is the ultimate store cupboard fail-safe, mid-week supper. Hot pasta is bathed in olive oil flecked with scraps of garlic and chilli and masses of chopped herbs: it is hot and fiery but addictive. Adding a hint of mint with the coriander seems to offset all the flavours while bringing them together. There are so many variations on this simple meal. Try it without the chilli and herbs, and if you are a garlic lover, try the garlic raw, allowing the heat of the pasta to encourage its aroma. It makes a difference, too, if it's made with fresh or dried chilli. In the summer it seems more appropriate to make it with fresh chilli and in the winter to bump up the heat with dried chilli. Ring the changes with different herbs. Flat leaf parsley is always good with garlic. Other herbs that go well in this dish, either alone or in a combination, are basil, mint and chives. Serve with a glass or two of red wine.

250g/8oz spaghetti
4 garlic cloves
1 red chilli or ½ tsp dried chilli flakes
30g/1½oz bunch coriander or flat leaf parsley

few mint leaves
6 tbsp olive oil
salt and freshly ground black pepper

Bring a large saucepan of water to the boil. Add salt and then the pasta and cook until *al dente* following the package instructions, usually about 12 minutes. Drain, saving about 2 tablespoons of cooking water. Return both the pasta and water to the pan and keep warm.

Meanwhile, peel the garlic and chop finely. Trim the chilli, split lengthways, scrape away the seeds, slice into skinny strips and then chop into tiny scraps. Discard the bulk of the coriander or parsley stalks. Add the mint leaves and chop the herbs together. When the pasta is ready, add the olive oil to a frying pan, warm through and add the garlic. Cook briefly, stirring constantly, for about 30 seconds and then add the chilli. Cook for a further 30 seconds until the garlic is patched very pale brown, but make sure it doesn't darken, or it will turn bitter. Add the contents of the garlic pan to the pasta together with the chopped herbs.

Toss thoroughly until all the pasta is sliding around in its delicious oil. Serve immediately. Do not be tempted to serve this with grated Parmesan or another cheese. There is enough going on without it.

Spanish lentil soup with green olives and pimiento

Serves 2–4 *20 minutes preparation: 40 minutes cooking*

Scrounging round the back of the food cupboard for something to liven up the end of a packet of Puy lentils led to this lovely soup. It gets its Spanish connection from those intensely flavoured Spanish roast piquillo pimientos (small, pointed red peppers), which are now widely available in supermarkets and delicatessens. The other Spanish ingredient is green olives. The soup smells wonderful as it cooks and looks cheerful and inviting with scraps of red pepper, lemon zest, green olives and flat leaf parsley bobbing around in the lentil-thick broth. Each mouthful is a lively contrast of creamy and sharp flavours and, like most lentil-based soups, it's extremely filling.

1 large red onion
3 garlic cloves
1 tbsp olive oil
½ tsp fresh thyme leaves or generous pinch dried
1 unwaxed lemon
10 large or 20 small green olives
4 roasted piquillo pimiento red peppers, sold in jars

100g/3½oz Puy lentils
½ tbsp flour
1 vegetable stock cube dissolved in 600ml/1 pint hot water
1 tbsp finely chopped flat leaf parsley
salt and freshly ground black pepper

Peel and halve the onion. Chop half and finely slice the other half. Peel and chop the garlic. Heat the olive oil in a medium-sized, heavy-based, lidded saucepan and stir in the onion, garlic and thyme. Cook briskly, stirring often, for about 8 minutes until the onion wilts and begins to brown.

Meanwhile, use a potato peeler to remove the zest from the lemon in wafer-thin, long sheets. Cut into chunky scraps. Give the olives a good bash with something heavy to loosen the stones and then tear or chop into pieces. Cut the peppers in half, open them out like a book and pile them on top of each other. Chop through the pile to make postage-stamp-sized pieces. Stir the lemon zest and then the lentils into the onion and cook, stirring constantly, for a couple of minutes. Now add the olives and peppers. Stir well, dust the surface with flour and quickly stir it into the lentils until it disappears.

Squeeze half the lemon into the lentils, add the stock and stir thoroughly while increasing the heat. Bring the soup to the boil. Reduce the heat slightly, cover the pan and leave to simmer for 30 minutes. Check the lentils are done, cooking for a few more minutes if they aren't, and adjust the seasoning with salt, pepper and lemon juice. Stir in the parsley and serve. If reheating, you may need to add extra liquid.

Squid-ink spaghetti with sun-blushed tomatoes

Serves 4   *15 minutes preparation: 15 minutes cooking*

Move over sun-dried tomatoes, there's a new kid on the block and it has various names. Sun-kissed or sun-blushed tomatoes have been slowly roasted in the oven until they are half dried and then submerged in olive oil. They are easy enough to make at home, left in the oven for an hour or two, but it's so convenient to have a shop-bought jar in the store cupboard for impromptu suppers like this one. These tomatoes succeed because they are instantly ready for use in risotto, pasta dishes, salads and tarts, imparting a similar concentrated tomato flavour to sun-dried but being soft and juicy without the need for rehydration. Non-vegetarians will love the black squid-ink spaghetti that makes this simple but delicious pasta supper stunning to look at – red, green and white against the black – and the hint of seafood complements the flavours. It is good too with ordinary spaghetti. Any leftovers are delicious warm or cold and perfect for the lunch box.

400g/14oz spaghetti
2 large garlic cloves
3 tbsp olive oil
75g/3oz piece Parmesan cheese

250g/8oz jar sun-blushed or sun-kissed tomatoes
 in olive oil
75g/3oz rocket
salt and freshly ground black pepper

Put a large saucepan of water on to boil. Salt generously and add the spaghetti. Boil for 10–15 minutes until just *al dente*. Drain. Meanwhile, crush the garlic with your fist and flake away the papery skin. Split the cloves lengthways and remove and discard the green germ growing in the middle. Chop the garlic, sprinkle with a little salt and use the flat of a knife to work it to a paste.

Pour the olive oil into the spaghetti pan, stir in the garlic and return to the heat, stirring constantly for about 30 seconds until aromatic but uncoloured. Add the tomatoes and their olive oil, stir around to heat through and then remove the pan from the heat.

Return the pasta, stir well. Cut the Parmesan cheese into flakes using a potato peeler, then add the rocket and Parmesan to the pan. Season with black pepper and toss again, until the rocket wilts and the Parmesan melts. Serve immediately.

Seafood

Whenever television chefs proclaim the virtues of seafood and show us how to cook it, my fishmonger does a roaring trade. On Friday – traditionally the British day for a fish supper – business is brisk and on Saturday, when the men folk go shopping, he sells more luxury seafood such as wild salmon, halibut and langoustine. The rest of the week, whatever the time of year, business is up and down. It's rare to see the sort of queues that are commonplace at the butcher.

Every day, bar Monday when most fish shops are closed, he lays out his display on the wet slab like a work of art. He orders his fish alphabetically, he tells me, before rattling off the briny litany of today's catch, but his display is a matter of what takes his fancy. Slippery, plump, pointed monkfish tails might line up next to handsome golden grey Dover soles or orange-spotted plaice. Stupendous whole codfish usually snuggle up to neatly sliced fillets and oval-shaped steaks that show the huge flakes of this dense, succulent fish. The mottled green-grey and golden skins of herrings, sardines and mackerel glint beguilingly next to the stupendous sight of a large salmon trout or a startlingly pink salmon tail. Less familiar fish, such as hoki and tilapia, and unfashionable huss (also known as many as dog fish, wolf fish or rock fish), look ordinary next to huge steaks of burgundy-red tuna. These in turn appear spookily unfishy against a neat pile of snowy-white squid, their tentacles alarmingly alien to many customers. In the shellfish corner there might be brown shrimps and pink prawns, mounds of blue-black mussels and dressed crab, the white and brown meat neatly separated and laid out in its shell. Often there are unfamiliar spider crabs, their huge, knobbly bodies resting on long, folded legs. Occasionally a browny-blue live lobster or crayfish, its claws safely ensnared in wide, blue rubber bands, sleepily surveys the scene. When there's an 'r' in the month, native oysters spill out of their traditional wooden barrel.

For customers like me, these displays are endlessly tempting. Part of the pleasure of these visits is watching my fishmonger choose a knife from his razor-sharp collection and with deft efficiency do whatever is necessary to render my choice ready for the pan. He decorates his piscatorial display with colourful plastic lobsters, fishnets and buoys. These are popular with small children who drag their mothers to the window and occasionally into the shop to get closer to the lobsters' faceted carapace and long, whiskery antennae.

The basic rule when buying fish, wherever it's from, is to look for bright, plump eyes, clear skin that is hard to the touch, a clean smell and bright red gills.

Fillets should feel firm, look clean and smell unfishy. Shellfish should have tightly shut shells and feel heavy and full. Whether your fish comes from a fishmonger (often family-run and with knowledgeable staff) or the supermarket (which has keen prices due to buying power but no specialist staff), it provides the perfect solution for the cook in a hurry who wants a healthy, nutritious meal. It is easy to cook in a variety of ways – poached, steamed, baked, stewed and fried – and offers a huge choice of textures and flavours. All fish, particularly oily fish like mackerel and tuna, are a good source of omega-3 fatty acids. These polyunsaturated fats make the blood less likely to clot, so people who eat fatty fish regularly have a lower risk of heart attack. It's also a good source of vitamins A and D, which strengthen hair, bones and teeth.

There is only one rule to remember about cooking fish: don't overcook.

After-work bouillabaisse

Serves 3–4   *15 minutes preparation: 20 minutes cooking*

It's the devil of a palaver to make a real bouillabaisse. The Mediterranean fisherman's soup was traditionally prepared with fish left behind in the nets, but has ended up being a soup of romance and mystery surrounded by legend and hearsay. This basic version dispenses with the elaborate fish stock, but includes the saffron which gives the soup its distinctive aroma and flavour, not to mention a yellow colour. Any firm white fish is perfect, and a mixture would be just dandy. The prawns add colour and a welcome change of texture. This big soup is healthy and low in calories. For a perfectly balanced meal, serve it with a handful of lightly cooked green beans.

12 medium-sized waxy variety or new potatoes
1 onion
2 garlic cloves
2 tbsp olive oil
1 large fennel bulb
3 plum tomatoes
strip orange zest, 5 x 1cm/2 x ½in long

½ chicken stock cube
pinch saffron
400g/14oz cod, haddock, pollock or other thick, firm white fish fillets
175g/6oz raw or cooked king prawns
small bunch flat leaf parsley
salt and freshly ground black pepper

Put the unpeeled potatoes on to boil in plenty of salted water. When tender to the point of a knife, drain the potatoes, return them to the pan and cover with cold water. Leave for a minute or so to cool, drain again and remove the skins. Halve the potatoes. Meanwhile, peel and finely chop the onion. Peel the garlic, chop coarsely and sprinkle with ½ teaspoon salt. Crush in a pestle and mortar or using the flat of a knife to make a juicy paste.

Heat the oil in a large frying pan or similarly wide-based pan and stir in the onion and then the garlic. Sauté gently, stirring often, for about 5 minutes without letting the onion brown. Split the fennel bulb, cut out the dense core and slice across the layers very finely, reserving the fronds. Add the fennel to the onion, increase the heat slightly and then cook for a further 5 minutes.

Meanwhile, pour boiling water over the tomatoes, count to 20, drain and remove the skin. Chop the tomatoes. Add the tomatoes, orange zest and a generous pinch of salt to the pan together with a generous grinding of black pepper. Let the vegetables simmer gently for 6–7 minutes, or until almost soft. Dissolve the stock cube in 350ml/12fl oz boiling water and stir in the saffron. Pour onto the vegetables and bring to the boil.

Simmer for a couple of minutes while you slice the fish into 2.5cm/1in wide chunks. Check the seasoning of the liquids, then slip in the pieces of fish so they are covered. Cook for 2–3 minutes until the fish has turned white and opaque. Add the prawns and potatoes and warm through. If using raw prawns, cook slightly longer until bright pink. Chop the fennel fronds and parsley leaves, sprinkle over the top of the soup and serve.

Clams with tomato and linguine

Serves 4   *25 minutes preparation: 20 minutes cooking*

Lido Azzurro is a modest but spectacularly located seafood restaurant on Italy's Amalfi coast. The dishes are simple, rely on the best and freshest ingredients, and the service is friendly and efficient. This was my first encounter with coal-black squid-ink bread, a wonderful trend just waiting to happen elsewhere. Imagine serving your crostini and bruschetta on black toast piled with snowy mozzarella and slippery roasted red peppers. I loved the simplicity of tossing baby shrimps with rocket, lemon juice and olive oil and seasoning crab with nothing more than lemon juice and grassy olive oil. This is my interpretation of a clam soup from this charming place. They serve it with lightly toasted bread to dip into the juices.

1kg/2lb clams	25g/1oz bunch flat leaf parsley
400g/14oz linguine	500g/1lb vine tomatoes
1 tbsp olive oil	50g/2oz butter
1 onion	1 tsp chopped thyme
4 garlic cloves	300ml/½ pint white wine
1 red chilli	salt and freshly ground black pepper

Place the clams in a sink full of cold water and agitate with your hands. Use a nail brush to give each one a quick but thorough scrub. Drain away the water, refill the sink and agitate again, drain and rinse until the water runs clean. Scoop the clams into a colander to drain. Discard any that remain open after tapping with a knife.

Put a large saucepan of water on to boil for the pasta and cook according to the packet instructions. Drain, toss with the olive oil and return to a large, warmed bowl. Cover and keep warm. Meanwhile, peel and finely chop the onion and garlic. Trim and split the chilli and scrape away the seeds. Slice the halves into skinny strips and then chop into tiny dice. Coarsely chop the parsley. Pour boiling water over the tomatoes. Count to 20, drain and splash with cold water. Remove the skins, quarter, scrape away the seeds and chop the flesh.

Melt 25g/1oz of the butter in the pan, placed over a medium-low heat. Add the garlic, onion, chilli and thyme and cook, stirring frequently, adjusting the heat as necessary, for 6–7 minutes, or until the onions are soft but not browned. Add the clams and wine. Increase the heat, cover the pan and boil for about 3 minutes or until all the clams open. Discard any that remain closed. Remove the clams with a slotted spoon and keep to one side.

Quickly reduce the liquid in the pan by half by boiling hard without a lid. Lower the heat, add the tomato dice and stir in the remaining butter. Stir the clams into the hot sauce, then tip into the pasta. Add the parsley, season with salt and plenty of black pepper, toss and serve.

Cod with white beans

Serves 2   *15 minutes preparation: 25 minutes cooking*

I feel a twinge of guilt every time I suggest a recipe using cod, particularly after headlines predicting its disappearance from the North Sea due to over-fishing. Some of the finest cod I've eaten recently came from Norway. It's fished in the deep, clear waters of the Barents Sea above the Arctic Circle and careful management and advanced fishing techniques mean the supply is reliable and consistent. It's noticeable for the thick, large fillets which fall into the characteristically big flakes of dense pearly white fish when cooked. Dishes like this show the incredible versatility of cod. Be sure not to overcook it; the minute the flesh turns opaque and comes away easily with your fork, it's ready.

3 rashers rindless streaky bacon
1 tbsp cooking oil
1 medium onion
400g/14oz can white haricot or cannellini beans
1 large garlic clove
1 lemon

½ chicken stock cube
Tabasco sauce
2 tomatoes, preferably plum
handful flat leaf parsley
250g/8oz thick cod, haddock or pollock fillet
salt and freshly ground black pepper

Slice across the bacon rashers to make little strips. Heat the oil in a medium-sized heavy-based saucepan and cook the bacon until crisp. Peel and finely chop the onion. Add it to the bacon and cook for 5–6 minutes until tender and lightly browned.

Tip the beans into a sieve, rinse with cold water and shake dry. Peel the garlic and chop it very finely. Remove the lemon zest in wafer-thin sheets and chop very finely. Stir this and the garlic into the pan and cook for a minute or so until aromatic. Add the beans and season generously with pepper and lightly with salt. Dissolve the stock cube in 250ml/8fl oz boiling water to make the stock. Add it and a generous splash of Tabasco to the pan. Simmer briskly for 5 minutes.

Meanwhile, cover the tomatoes with boiling water, count to 20, drain and peel. Coarsely chop the parsley. Cut the fish into big bite-sized chunks and season with salt and pepper. Stir the tomatoes and most of the parsley into the beans. Cook for a further 2 minutes, then stir in the fish, making sure it's all submerged. Cook for 5–10 minutes until the fish is opaque.

Check the seasoning: you may need a little more Tabasco or a squeeze of lemon and extra salt and pepper. Serve in shallow soup bowls with the last of the parsley and a wedge of lemon.

Cod with tomatoes, peppers and black olives

Serves 2   *15 minutes preparation: 20 minutes cooking*

If using frozen cod fillets for this light yet deliciously satisfying quick fish supper, a useful tip is to sprinkle the defrosted fish with a little salt and leave it for a few minutes before cooking. This has the double effect of drawing out excess water and firming up the fish. It also means the fish is seasoned right through the fillet. I love this sauce-cum-salsa and thick flakes of creamy cod with crusty bread, but rice or, if you prefer, boiled, crushed or mashed potato with lightly cooked green beans would be good too.

4 frozen cod steaks 300g/11oz total weight or	375g/12oz tomatoes
2 large fillets 125g/4oz each	1 tbsp tomato purée
1 large red onion	8 pitted black olives
1 plump garlic clove	handful flat leaf parsley
3 tbsp olive oil	flour for dusting
75g/3oz roasted red pepper from a jar	salt and freshly ground black pepper

If using frozen cod steaks, leave to defrost or speed things up by soaking in cold water for about 10 minutes. Peel, halve and finely chop the onion. Peel the garlic and slice in super-thin rounds. Heat 2 tablespoons of the oil in a frying pan and, when very hot, stir in the onion and garlic. Cook, stirring often, for at least 5 minutes, adjusting the heat so that the onion softens without crisping.

Meanwhile, slice the red pepper into ribbons and then into short strips. Pour boiling water over the tomatoes. Count to 20, drain, cut out the core and remove the skin. Coarsely chop the tomatoes. Stir the tomatoes and red pepper into the onion. Season generously with salt and pepper, stir in the tomato purée and cook for 5 minutes. Tear the olives into 2 or 3 pieces each and stir them in too, cooking for a further couple of minutes. Taste and adjust the seasoning. Coarsely chop the parsley and stir into the sauce. Transfer the sauce to a bowl and keep warm.

Give the fish a gentle squeeze to remove excess water. Pat dry on absorbent kitchen paper. Dust the fish with flour and shake away any excess. Heat the remaining oil in the pan and, when hot, quickly fry the fish for about 30 seconds a side. Spoon the sauce over the fish in the pan, heat through, then divide between two warmed plates.

Crab and cucumber linguine

Serves 4–6   *20 minutes preparation: 15 minutes cooking*

White crab meat simply dressed with lemon juice, olive oil and chopped flat leaf parsley is a wonderful combination. It makes a deliciously indulgent home-alone supper piled onto bruschetta made by toasting thick slices of sourdough bread, rubbing it with garlic and generously smearing it with olive oil. A good addition, which makes the crab go further and lends a crisp, clean flavour and crunchy texture, is thin slices of peeled and seeded cucumber. Adding a few scraps of finely chopped red chilli lifts the flavours in an exciting and delicious way. If you want to share your feast with friends, the crab mixture is terrific when mixed into hot linguine. Linguine is the pasta of the moment and, although it is similar to spaghetti, its firmer texture and thinner strands give exactly the right sort of resistance to the bite against the silky-white crab meat and thin slices of peeled cucumber which wilt against its heat. Serve this lovely summer pasta supper with a glass of chilled white wine. It is rich and luscious; do not be tempted to serve it with Parmesan or any other grated cheese.

400g/14oz linguine
1 tsp dried red chilli flakes or 2 fresh red chillies
1 small or ½ large cucumber
2 large dressed crabs and 6 large claws, yielding
  about 250g/8oz brown meat and 200g/7oz white

juice 2 large lemons
2 tbsp coarsely chopped flat-leaf parsley
6–8 tbsp extra virgin olive oil
sea salt and freshly ground black pepper

Put a large saucepan of water on to boil. Cook the pasta until it is *al dente*, then drain and return to the saucepan. Meanwhile, place the chilli flakes in an egg cup, just cover with boiling water and leave for a few minutes until soft. If using fresh chillies, trim and split them, scraping away the seeds. Slice into skinny strips and then into tiny dice.

Remove the skin from the cucumber with a potato peeler. Split it in half lengthways and use a teaspoon to scrape out the seeds and their watery surround. Thinly slice the cucumber into half moons. In a bowl, mix together the drained chilli flakes or fresh chilli, dressed crab, juice from 1½ of the lemons and the chopped parsley and season lightly with salt and generously with pepper. Crack the crab claws and scrape the meat off the flat central 'bone', leaving it in big chunks, directly into the mixture. Slowly stir in 4 tablespoons of the olive oil to make a thick but slack mixture.

Stir the cucumber and 2 tablespoons of the olive oil into the drained pasta, stirring to mix thoroughly and encouraging the cucumber to wilt slightly. Now add the crab mixture, adding more lemon juice or oil to taste. Serve with forks and spoons.

Crab jambalaya

Serves 6 *30 minutes preparation: 45 minutes cooking*

My mother-in-law, Betty John, was a terrific cook. She had what they call in Trinidad a 'sweet hand', able to make something special out of quite ordinary ingredients and unfazed by unexpected guests. This was one of her specialities that she made regularly with the crabs at her disposal in the Cornish fishing village where she lived. I made it twice recently, both times doing it from scratch, boiling and picking the crabs, then making stock with the remains, using basmati rice on one occasion and risotto rice on another. Proper crab stock obviously gives the dish a superb depth of flavour, and picking the crabs yourself means that the white crab meat can be left in delicious big lumps. This quickie version using dressed crab and stock cubes or a jar of Mediterranean fish soup is pretty good, too, although you might want to buy a few crab claws to add textural interest. Serve the jambalaya risotto-style; I quite like green beans on the side.

2 red onions
2 garlic cloves
2 tbsp vegetable oil
2 red peppers
1 bay leaf
3 dried chillies
250g/8oz basmati rice
400g/14oz fresh tomatoes or 400g/14oz can
  skinless cherry tomatoes

3 dressed crabs, yielding about 250g/8oz brown
  meat and 200g/7oz white
600ml/1 pint chicken or fish stock (cubes are fine)
  or jar Mediterranean fish soup
1 small lemon
Tabasco sauce
salt and freshly ground black pepper
2 tbsp chopped flat leaf parsley

Peel and dice the onions and garlic. Heat the oil in large frying pan or similarly wide-based saucepan and stir in the onions and garlic. Cook gently for 5 minutes or so while you dice the red peppers, discarding seeds, white membrane and stalk. Stir the peppers into the onions, together with the bay leaf and chillies, cooking for about 15 minutes until the onions are soft and slippery, the peppers partially softened and the chillies crumbled.

Meanwhile, rinse the rice in several changes of water. If using fresh tomatoes, place them in a bowl and cover with boiling water. Count to 20, drain, remove the skins, cut out the core and coarsely chop them. Stir the rice into the vegetables in the pan and then add the brown crab meat. Cook for a couple of minutes, then add the tomatoes and their juices, ½ teaspoon salt and plenty of pepper. Now add the stock or fish soup and bring the liquid to the boil, stir, reduce the heat, cover the pan and cook for 15 minutes.

Turn off the heat and leave the pan without removing the lid – the rice will finish cooking in the steam generated – for 10 minutes. Stir in the white crab meat. Taste the juices, adjust the seasoning with salt, pepper and lemon juice, adding a shake or two of Tabasco if it isn't hot enough. Stir in the parsley and serve.

Leek salad with pilchards and balsamic dressing

Serves 2 *10 minutes preparation: 15 minutes cooking*

Pilchards are grown-up sardines and a speciality of Cornwall. Sadly, they have never caught on, either canned or fresh, in the same way as sardines or their relative the mackerel, but there are moves afoot to widen the appeal of Cornish pilchards. The canning process has been brought into line with that of the finest sardines and tuna, by first filleting the fish and flash-frying them before they are canned in extra virgin olive oil. If you can find these tasty morsels, they work wonderfully well in this light and healthy salad supper, but if not, so too do tuna fillets. With plenty of crusty bread and butter, the salad is satisfying enough as a main course, but if you have big appetites, start with soup or finish with a hot pudding such as treacle tart and custard.

2 trimmed leeks, about 300g/10oz
150g/5oz extra fine green beans
2 eggs, hard-boiled
100g/3½oz can Cornish pilchard fillets or
   65g/2½oz can tuna fillets, oil reserved

150g/5oz cherry tomatoes
1 tbsp aged balsamic vinegar
2 tbsp extra virgin olive oil
1 tbsp finely chopped chives
salt and freshly ground black pepper

Cut the leeks into 3–4 10cm/4in lengths. Bring a large saucepan of water to the boil, salt generously and add the leeks. Return the water to the boil, cover the pan and boil for about 5 minutes or until the leeks are cooked through and can be pierced easily with a sharp knife. Scoop the leeks into a colander, upending them to drain and cool. Top and tail the beans, cut them in half and add them to the boiling leeks water. Return to the boil and boil for 2–3 minutes until just *al dente*. Drain.

Meanwhile, peel the eggs and quarter lengthways. Halve the tomatoes round their middles. Gently squeeze the leeks to remove any trapped water and remove the outer layer if it seems a bit crusty.

Arrange the leeks on two dinner plates. Cover with a share of the beans and scatter the tomatoes over the top. Arrange the pilchard or tuna fillets over the salad and add the eggs. Season with black pepper and balsamic vinegar. Dribble the oil from the fish can over the salad, adding some of the extra virgin olive oil if necessary. Scatter the chives over the top and serve.

Monkfish chowder with green beans and thyme

Serves 2   *20 minutes preparation: 30 minutes cooking*

There couldn't be a much simpler and quicker way of making a comforting and satisfying yet chic and healthy fish supper than this soup-cum-stew. It's roughly based on a New England chowder. These chunky soups usually contain seafood and potatoes and are always made with milk. If you are a meat eater, a good way of perking up a homely soup like this is with a few scraps of crispy fried bacon. Cook it right at the beginning, then remove when nicely crisped, leaving behind a smoky bacon flavour. Sprinkled over the top with the parsley, it makes a delicious salty garnish. If buying monkfish from a fishmonger, be sure to ask him to remove the slippery membrane that covers the fish fillets, and if buying from a supermarket, check that it has been removed. If left intact, it will shrink and turn horribly rubbery during the cooking. This lovely soup is plenty for two as a main dish and sufficient for four if followed with something else. Serve with crusty bread and butter for dunking.

625g/1¼lb new potatoes
500g/1lb monkfish fillet
1 leek, about 125g/4oz
1 shallot
25g/1oz butter
1 sprig thyme

1 bay leaf
100g/3½oz green beans (extra fine if possible)
400ml/14fl oz milk
1 tbsp finely chopped flat leaf parsley
salt and freshly ground black pepper

Boil the unpeeled potatoes in plenty of salted water until tender. Drain, return to the pan, cover with cold water and leave for a couple of minutes. Drain again, remove the skins and cut into chunks. Meanwhile, cut the monkfish into small kebab-sized chunks. Trim the leek, split lengthways and then slice across the leek to make chunky half moons. Tip into a colander, rinse under cold water and shake dry. Trim, peel and finely chop the shallot.

Melt the butter in a heavy-based, lidded saucepan placed over a medium-low heat. Stir in the leek and shallot. Add a generous seasoning of salt and pepper, the thyme and bay leaf. Adjust the heat so that the vegetables soften gently, cover the pan and cook for 10 minutes. Top and tail the beans, then cut them in half. Stir the beans into the leek and shallot, cover the pan and cook, stirring a couple of times, for a further 5 minutes.

Now add the fish. Stir as it firms and turns snowy white. Add the potatoes and milk. Simmer for about 10 minutes to finish cooking the fish. Taste and adjust the seasoning. Remove the thyme and bay leaf, sprinkle with the chopped parsley and serve.

Pan-fried salmon tabbouleh

Serves 6   *30 minutes preparation: 10 minutes cooking*

Tabbouleh is the name of a Lebanese cracked wheat salad with a high proportion of flat leaf parsley and tomatoes. In this salmon version, big chunks of crusty pan-fried salmon are folded into the olive-oil-and-lemon-tossed salad, together with a handful of young spinach, some mint and finely sliced spring onions. It is extremely simple to make and tastes as lively and attractive as it looks. As with most cracked wheat and couscous salads, it doesn't matter a jot if some ingredients are hot and others are warm or cold.

175g/6oz bulgar cracked wheat
4 firm vine tomatoes, approx 400g/14oz
125g/4oz spring onions
juice 1 lemon
125ml/4fl oz olive oil

1 large bunch flat leaf parsley, at least 75g/3oz
large handful mint leaves
100g/3½oz small young spinach leaves
4 fresh salmon fillets, skinned
salt and freshly ground black pepper

Boil the kettle and measure off 300ml/½ pint water into a mixing bowl. Add the bulgar. Cover the dish and leave to soak for 15 minutes while you place a sieve over a bowl and quarter the tomatoes lengthways. Scrape the seeds and juices into the sieve. Using the back of a spoon, press the seeds and juices against the side of the sieve to extract the maximum juice.

Coarsely chop the tomatoes. Trim and finely slice the spring onions. Whisk together the tomato juice, lemon juice and olive oil. Season generously with salt and pepper and stir the mixture into the bulgar. Stir in the spring onions and then the tomatoes. Pick the leaves off the parsley stalks and chop. Shred the mint leaves. Stir both into the bulgar. Add the spinach and stir again.

Now cook the salmon. Heat a non-stick frying pan over a medium heat. If you wish, paint the fish with a little cooking oil, although the heat will release the fish's natural oils. Arrange the salmon in the pan. Cook for 2 minutes a side, pressing down to encourage crusty edges and until just cooked but still moist. Lift out of the pan and allow to cool. Flake the fish into ragged chunks. Gently mix the fish into the salad and serve.

Mussels with coconut cream, chilli and coriander

Serves 2–4   *15 minutes preparation: 20 minutes cooking*

As a general rule, the time to eat oysters and mussels is when there is an 'r' in the month and September is generally regarded as the start of the season. Dealing with oysters is best left to the experts, but preparing mussels is child's play. These days their beautiful black-blue shells come relatively clean and they are ready for the pot in minutes. This is a Thai-style take on moules marinière *and the resultant broth has the hallmarks of a coconut-milk Thai soup, being all at once creamy, sour, chilli-hot and citrus-scented. Serve with crusty bread; I think there is plenty here for four big appetites, but the mussels are very more-ish.*

2kg/4lb mussels
1 red onion
1 small unwaxed lemon
3 garlic cloves
2 small red chillies

2 tbsp vegetable oil
2 tbsp Thai fish sauce (*nam pla*)
200ml/7fl oz coconut cream
50g/2oz bunch coriander
freshly ground black pepper

Tip the mussels into a sink of cold water and agitate thoroughly, repeating a couple of times until the water runs clean. Discard any mussels that are cracked or open. Pull off the 'beards' and discard. Leave the mussels in a colander to finish draining while you prepare the broth. Peel, halve and finely chop the onion. Using a zester or potato peeler, remove the zest from half the lemon in paper-thin strips and chop quite small. Peel and finely chop the garlic. Trim and split the chillies, scrape away the seeds, slice into thin strips and then across into tiny scraps. Don't forget to wash your hands to remove the chilli juice, which burns sensitive areas.

Heat the oil in a large saucepan with a well-fitting lid. Stir in the onion, lemon zest, garlic and chilli and cook, adjusting the heat so nothing burns, for 6–7 minutes until the onion is tender. Add the fish sauce, coconut cream and juice from half of the lemon. Season generously with black pepper. Chop the coriander, including the stalks, which should be sliced very finely, and add half of the bunch (including stalks) to the pan. Simmer for a couple of minutes, taste and adjust the seasoning with lemon juice.

Tip the drained mussels into the pan, stir a couple of times with a wooden spoon, clamp on the lid and cook at a high heat for 5 minutes. Lift off the lid, check if the mussels are opening – it doesn't take long – and give the pan a good shake or another stir, trying to bring the already opened mussels on the bottom to the top. Replace the lid and cook for a few more minutes. Check again that all the mussels are open, returning the lid for a couple more minutes if necessary, add the rest of the coriander, give a final stir and then tip the contents of the pan into a warmed bowl. Discard any mussels which haven't opened.

Pad Thai

Serves 4   *15 minutes preparation: 10 minutes cooking*

Pad Thai is the noodle dish that everyone loves. A good one, when the noodles are silky and moist with their delicious garlicky, sweet-and-sour sauce, and the pile is well-loaded with prawns and other titbits, is hard to resist. My version is generous with the chopped peanuts, fresh coriander and sliced spring onion, with several wedges of lime or lemon. You can probably buy everything you need at the supermarket but, if you are lucky enough to have one nearby, it is much more fun shopping for the authentic ingredients at a Thai store, and the families who run them tend to be incredibly helpful.

200g/7oz medium egg noodles
3 tbsp sweet chilli sauce
3 tbsp Thai fish sauce (*nam pla*)
3 tbsp vegetable oil
3 large garlic cloves
200g/7oz raw headless Tiger prawns or cooked
  peeled large prawns
200ml7fl oz carton coconut cream

½ tbsp shrimp paste
2 large eggs
2 spring onions
2 tbsp salted roasted peanuts
200g/7oz bean sprouts
2 tbsp coriander leaves
2 limes or lemons, cut into wedges

As always with a stir-fry, get everything laid out and ready, preferably in the order that it is going to hit the pan, before you start cooking. Place the noodles in large pan and cover with boiling water. Return to the boil, then leave to soak for 4 minutes. Drain and toss with the chilli sauce mixed with the fish sauce and 1 tablespoon of the oil. Peel and finely chop the garlic. If using raw prawns, peel them but leave the tail ends intact. Run a sharp knife down their curled backs, cutting less than half-way through.

Heat the coconut cream and shrimp paste in a small saucepan, stirring until smooth and hot. Add the raw or cooked prawns. If using raw prawns, cook gently for a couple of minutes until pink and cooked through. Whisk the eggs in a bowl with ½ tablespoon of the oil. Finely slice the spring onions on the slant. Coarsely grind the peanuts in a blender or food processor.

Heat the wok, add the remaining oil, swirling it round the pan. Add the garlic, frying for about 30 seconds until golden. Add the eggs, letting them set, then stir to scramble. Add the noodles and toss and stir for a couple of minutes. Add the prawns and coconut mix, tossing thoroughly and breaking down the scrambled egg against the noodles and prawns. Add the bean sprouts and stir-fry until barely cooked.

Pile the Pad Thai onto a platter and strew with the spring onions, coriander leaves and peanuts. Edge with the lime or lemon wedges and serve.

Potato gnocchi with prawns and minted peas

Serves 2 *10 minutes preparation: 15 minutes cooking*

This classy little number is the perfect smart comfort supper for two. It ends up risotto-like, the starch from the gnocchi slightly thickening the white-wine juices. It is similarly more-ish and very satisfying. Serve it with ciabatta or another crusty bread and some decent butter. Drink the rest of the bottle of wine with the meal.

400g/14oz ready-made potato gnocchi
125g/4oz spring onions
50g/2oz butter
150g/5oz frozen petits pois
large glass white wine, about 175ml/6fl oz

200g/7oz cooked peeled large prawns
2 tbsp chopped mint
2 tbsp grated Parmesan cheese
salt and freshly ground black pepper

Put a large frying pan or similar-sized wide-based pan of water on to boil. Add the gnocchi and plenty of salt and return to the boil. The gnocchi are done when they've all risen to the surface. Drain.

Trim and finely slice the spring onions. Melt the butter in the pan and soften the spring onions. After about 5 minutes add the frozen peas. Season with salt and pepper and cook for 2–3 minutes until the peas are tender and the onions very soft. Add the white wine, stir well and return the gnocchi. Bubble steadily for several minutes to reduce slightly and infuse the gnocchi with the flavour, then stir in the prawns.

Cook until the prawns are hot. Taste and adjust the seasoning with salt and pepper, then stir in the chopped mint. Dust with the Parmesan and serve.

Caesar salad with smoked salmon

Serves 2   *15 minutes preparation: 5 minutes cooking*

One of the most popular lunch dishes at the Porthgwidden Beach Café in St Ives, Cornwall, on one of the hottest days of summer was Caesar salad with smoked salmon. All around me, as I picked my way through the limited menu which had been reduced by a freak power cut, there were people tucking into deep, white bowls full of tall, pointy leaves draped with smoked salmon. I copied the idea at home and also made it very successfully with flaked honey-roast Scottish salmon. I cheated with the dressing and stirred anchovy paste into mayonnaise let down with olive oil and wine vinegar, but made my own chunky and very crusty croutons. I copied the Café and included a few strips of Parma ham and flakes of Parmesan – easy to achieve by taking a potato peeler to a chunk of Parmesan. Serve it with crusty bread and butter.

4 slices ciabatta bread or 8 slices baguette
4 tbsp olive oil
1 tbsp mayonnaise
1 tbsp anchovy paste
½ tbsp red wine vinegar

2 baby Cos or Romaine lettuces or 4 Little Gem
   lettuce hearts
125g/4oz honey-roast salmon flakes or
   150g/5oz smoked salmon trimmings
2 slices Parma ham
10 Parmesan cheese flakes

Cut the bread into postage-stamp-sized pieces without removing the crusts. Heat 3 tablespoons of the oil in a frying pan and, when hot, add the bread, immediately tossing it around so all the pieces get a share of oil. Cook briskly until golden on both sides. Tip onto kitchen paper to drain.

Place the mayonnaise in a deep salad bowl. Stir in the anchovy paste, remaining olive oil and red wine vinegar, adding 1 tablespoon water if it seems too thick. Separate the lettuce leaves, rinse and shake dry. Stir the lettuce into the dressing. Add the flaked fish or scraps of smoked salmon, the Parma ham, torn into strips, the Parmesan flakes and drained croûtons. Toss again. Serve immediately.

Squid or scallop provençale with basmati rice

Serves 2–4   *15 minutes preparation: 15 minutes cooking*

This is a sure-fire winner of a recipe and makes the perfect quick and healthy spring supper. If you are not sure about squid, try it with prawns or, if money is no object, scallops. Another option would be mussels, but these would have to be cooked first, then removed from their shells. Alternatively, it can be made with firm-fleshed fish such as monkfish. I find it tricky to predict how many the dish will feed because it is so easy to eat that everyone wants more than expected.

300g/10oz basmati rice
400g/14oz cleaned squid or scallops without shells
2 garlic cloves
250g/8oz cherry tomatoes
50g/2oz butter

1 tbsp olive oil
1½ lemons (½ for juice, 1 for wedges)
½ glass dry white wine
large bunch flat leaf parsley, at least 75g/3oz
salt and freshly ground black pepper

Rinse the rice until the water runs clean and place in a saucepan with a well-fitting lid with 450ml/¾ pint cold water. Bring to the boil, then reduce the heat to very low, cover the pan and cook for 10 minutes. Remove from the heat but leave the lid in place for a further 10 minutes so the rice finishes cooking in the steam.

Meanwhile, prepare the squid by slicing the sacs in chunky rings, approximately 1cm/½in wide. Squeeze out the hard mouth from the centre of the tentacles – it will pop out easily – and discard it with everything else. Divide the tentacles into 2 or 3 pieces each, depending on their size. If using scallops, separate the coral and slice the white part into rounds. Peel and chop the garlic, sprinkle with a generous pinch of salt and use the flat of a knife to crush to a juicy paste. Quarter the cherry tomatoes, then slice across the quarters.

Heat the butter and oil in a spacious frying pan, stir in the garlic and almost immediately the squid or scallops (if using scallops, add the coral for a minute first before adding the rest), moderating the heat so it cooks gently. After a couple of minutes, squeeze in the juice from the half lemon and then add the white wine. Let everything bubble up and add the tomatoes. Cook for 2–3 minutes to allow everything to mix and merge.

Pick the leaves off the parsley and coarsely chop; you need at least 4 heaped tablespoons. Stir the parsley into the dish before the tomatoes have had a chance to collapse. Season generously with black pepper and lightly with salt. Serve immediately over the rice with lemon wedges, accompanied by the rice.

Squid with tomatoes and green peas

Serves 2   *20 minutes preparation: 50 minutes cooking*

Few foods provoke such strong feelings, both for and against, as squid. They make people squeamish – the very same people, probably, who wolf down deep-fried calamari rings on their Spanish holiday. This is a pity because the snowy-white tube-like body of this under-rated mollusc is tender and sweet and comes without a shell. Most fishmongers will clean squid for you, but it's a painless and simple enough job if your fish supplier can't do it. Based on an old favourite recipe of Marcella Hazan's, this is a dish to convert would-be squid haters. It can be made up to 48 hours in advance and is best eaten with crusty bread to scoop up the juices.

1 onion
2 garlic cloves
2 tbsp olive oil
400g/14oz can chopped tomatoes

375g/12oz small squid, fresh or frozen, cleaned
200g/7oz frozen peas
salt and freshly ground black pepper
lemon wedges to serve

Peel, halve and finely chop the onion and garlic. Heat the oil in a heavy-based, medium-sized saucepan that can hold all the ingredients. Sauté the onion over a medium heat, stirring occasionally, for about 10 minutes until it begins to soften and turn golden. Add the garlic and cook for a couple of minutes before adding the tomatoes. Cook at a gentle simmer for about 15 minutes until the tomatoes begin to thicken and the onion melts into them to make a cohesive sauce.

Meanwhile, slice the squid sacs (its body) into 1cm/½in-wide rings. Cut off the tentacles. Squeeze out the hard mouth from the centre of the tentacles – it will pop out easily – and discard it with everything else. Divide the tentacle clusters in half. Add the rings and tentacles to the pan. Season with salt and pepper, stir well, cover and cook at a gentle simmer for about 20 minutes, or until the squid is tender. Taste and adjust the seasoning.

Stir in the peas and cook for a few minutes until they are done. If the sauce seems too dry – you want the dish to be juicy rather than wet – add a little water. Serve with lemon wedges.

Prawn laksa with green beans

Serves 4   *30 minutes preparation: 40 minutes cooking*

The point of Malaysian laksa is its finely balanced sweet, sour, hot and spicy coconut broth. Into this gorgeous liquor go prawns, bean sprouts and other vegetables to give crunch, and the 'soup' (which is more of a meal) is served over rice noodles. Traditionally, laksa is made with vermicelli-style rice noodles (sometimes sold as stir-fry rice noodles), but egg noodles are good too. It is a great thing to make when you have friends coming over because all preparation can be done in advance and the last-minute cooking is quick and mindless.

1kg/2lb raw king prawns, headless with shells on	1 tsp brown sugar
1 onion	2 limes (one for juice, 1 for wedges)
3 plump garlic cloves	400g/14oz can coconut milk
25g/1oz fresh ginger	2 tbsp vegetable oil
3 lemon grass stalks	150g/5oz trimmed French beans
bunch coriander with roots, at least 75g/3oz	200g/7oz dried stir-fry rice noodles
1 Scotch Bonnet chilli or 4 small red chillies	250g/8oz bean sprouts
6 macadamia nuts or 10 blanched almonds	125g/4oz bunch spring onions
1½ tsp each of ground coriander, cumin and turmeric	salt

If using frozen prawns, soak them in warm water to defrost. Drain, remove the shells and run a sharp knife down the back of each prawn to remove the black 'vein'. Place the shells in a saucepan with 750ml/1¼ pints water and simmer for 15 minutes. Discard the shells and simmer for 5 more minutes. Transfer the stock to a bowl or jug.

While the stock is cooking, peel and chop the onion, garlic and ginger. Peel the lemon grass to locate the tender inner shoot then chop. Remove 6 coriander roots with 5cm/2in of stem from the bunch. Place these prepared ingredients into the bowl of the food processor. Split, deseed and chop the chillies. Add the chilli, nuts, ground coriander, cumin, turmeric, sugar, teaspoon salt, the juice of 1 lime, 4 tablespoons of the coconut milk and the oil to the bowl. Blitz to make a red-flecked, yellow paste.

Refill the stock pan with water and put on to boil. Cut the beans in half and boil them for 30 seconds. Scoop the beans out of the pan and set aside. Put the noodles in a bowl and pour over the boiling water. Stir and leave the noodles to rehydrate according to packet instructions.

Simmer the spice paste in a large, heavy-based pan for 5 minutes. Gradually incorporate the prawn stock and remaining coconut milk. Simmer for 5 minutes, then add bean sprouts and prawns. Cook for 6–10 minutes or until the prawns are cooked. Trim and finely slice the spring onions and coarsely chop the remaining coriander leaves. Add the beans, spring onions and chopped coriander to the laksa. Drain the noodles, share between deep bowls and spoon over the laksa. Serve with lime wedges.

Smoked mackerel noodles with horseradish cream

Serves 4   *15 minutes preparation: 15 minutes cooking*

When you're whizzing round the supermarket, looking for something quick and easy yet unusual and impressive to make for friends for a weekday supper, smoked mackerel isn't the obvious choice. This fusion of flavours will change your mind: a soy-seasoned broth with onions, carrots, beans and pickled ginger alongside Chinese noodles and coriander makes a good backdrop for this meaty and robustly flavoured fish. The idea comes from one of my sons, who cooked something similar for me for supper recently. It was so good, I had to have a go myself. Do give it a try; it's simple, the ingredients are easy to shop for and the dish is very economical. Perfect.

2 onions
3 tbsp vegetable oil
2 garlic cloves
1 small red chilli
4 carrots
150g/5oz fine green beans
1½ chicken stock cubes

3 tbsp soy sauce
250g/8oz medium egg noodles
handful coriander leaves
50g/2oz pickled sushi ginger (see page 66)
4 smoked mackerel fillets
4 tbsp creamed horseradish
salt

Peel, halve and finely slice the onions. Heat the oil in a spacious saucepan over a medium heat and stir in the onions. Cook, stirring occasionally, for 5 minutes until floppy but not browned. Peel the garlic and slice in wafer-thin rounds. Trim the chilli, split lengthways, scrape away the seeds, slice into skinny batons and then into tiny dice. Stir the garlic and chilli into the onions and cook for a couple of minutes.

Trim and peel the carrots, then slice thinly, cutting on the slant. Stir the carrots into the onions, season lightly with salt and cook and continue stirring for another couple of minutes. Trim and halve the beans. Dissolve the stock cubes in 750ml/1¼ pints boiling water. Add the soy sauce, then pour into the pan. Increase the heat and bring the liquid to the boil. Add the beans to the boiling stock, return to the boil and cook for 2–3 minutes until the beans are just tender.

Co-ordinate cooking the noodles according to the packet instructions – mine took 4 minutes – to be ready now. Drain. Coarsely chop the coriander and stir it together with the pickled ginger into the broth. Break the mackerel off its skin in bite-sized chunks and add that too, letting it warm through. Serve the noodles in soup bowls, spoon over the broth with the vegetables and fish and garnish with a dollop of horseradish cream.

Tagliatelle with smoked salmon and chives

Serves 2   *10 minutes preparation: 15 minutes cooking*

Not so long ago smoked salmon was very posh and the only way we thought of eating it was with brown bread and butter. These days, now that salmon has taken over from cod as the most popular and accessible fish, smoked salmon is common too. It's available in packs of all sizes from off-cuts and special sandwich slices to half sides, neatly sliced and laid back in their original shape. It's on sale everywhere and quality, inevitably, is variable. As is increasingly evident with all food, you get what you pay for. As an after-work, quick supper ingredient it's a godsend. It suits all weather conditions and can be snacky or quickly worked up into more of a meal. Try it, for example, with blinis or hot tortillas with a dollop of crème fraîche stirred with creamed horseradish and a few rashers of crisp pancetta. Or with a simple potato salad tossed with olive oil, white wine vinegar and lots of chopped dill. It is terrific, too, with pasta. For a super-quickie version of this recipe, just stir crème fraîche or something similar into cooked pasta, toss with chives and serve draped with smoked salmon and a lemon wedge.

200g/7oz tagliatelle or fettucine
1 shallot
1 large unwaxed lemon
100g/3½oz smoked salmon or trout
50g/2oz butter

½ glass dry white wine, about 100ml/3½fl oz
100ml/3½fl oz crème fraîche
small bunch chives
salt and freshly ground black pepper

Cook the tagliatelle or fettucine according to the packet instructions in plenty of salted boiling water until *al dente*. Drain and return to the pan with a couple of tablespoons of the cooking water. Toss and keep warm.

Meanwhile, peel, halve and finely chop the shallot. Using a zester or potato peeler, remove the zest from half the lemon in paper-thin strips (reserve the rest for wedges). Chop quite small. Slice the salmon or trout into strips. Melt the butter in small frying pan or saucepan and stir in the shallot and chopped lemon zest. Cook gently, stirring often, for 5–6 minutes, or until the shallot is tender. Add the wine and boil for a couple of minutes until reduced slightly, then stir in the crème fraîche. Cook for a couple more minutes and stir in the salmon and most of the chives.

Heat through, then tip the contents of the pan into the pasta. Season generously with black pepper, toss well and serve with a garnish of chives and lemon wedges for squeezing on top.

Thai prawn salad with cucumber

Serves 2   *30 minutes preparation: 5 minutes cooking*

A crisp, vital salad to wake up the taste buds. Serve it alone or with basmati rice. Handily, at least one spice company sells fresh tamarind in 100g/3½oz jars, which are widely available.

1 lime
200g/7oz raw headless tiger prawns
1 red onion
150g/5oz green beans
½ large cucumber or 1 small one
2 Little Gem lettuce hearts
2 lemon grass stalks
3 large garlic cloves

3 red chillies
3 tsp fresh tamarind
2 tbsp Thai fish sauce (*nam pla*)
½ tbsp cooking oil
about 30 fresh mint leaves
small handful coriander leaves
salt

Remove the zest from the lime in paper-thin sheets and set aside. If the prawns are frozen, slip them into a bowl of warm water and leave for 5–6 minutes to defrost. Remove the shells. Run a sharp knife down the back of each prawn vein and remove the black membrane within. Place the prawns in a bowl and squeeze over the lime juice. Toss well so the prawns are thoroughly seasoned and leave for 10 minutes, then lift them out of the bowl and transfer to a plate.

Peel, halve and finely slice the red onion. Mix the slices into the lime juice and leave to marinate while you prepare the rest of the salad. Boil a medium-sized saucepan of water. Top, tail and halve the beans. Add salt and the beans to the boiling water, return to the boil and boil for 2 minutes. Drain and splash with cold water to arrest the cooking. Meanwhile, peel the cucumber and split it in half lengthways. Scrape out the seeds and the watery pulp and slice across the cucumber to make thin half moons. Unfurl the lettuce, wash and shake dry.

To make the salad dressing, place half the lime zest in the bowl of a liquidizer. Peel the outer layers of the lemon grass to reveal the tender inner shoot. Chop it coarsely. Flake away the papery skin of the garlic. Trim and split the chillies, scrape away the seeds and chop coarsely. Add the lemon grass, garlic and chillies to the lime zest together with the tamarind and fish sauce. Drain the lime juice from the red onions into the bowl. Liquidize to a smooth sauce-cum-dressing. If it seems stiff, add 1 tablespoon cold water. Transfer to a mixing bowl.

Heat the oil in a wok or large frying pan over a medium heat. Add the prawns and stir-fry for a couple of minutes until just cooked, turning from grey to pink. Stir the hot prawns into the dressing. Add the beans and cucumber. Arrange the lettuce leaves on a platter or in a large, shallow bowl. Coarsely chop the mint and coriander and scatter half over the lettuce. Spoon the prawn mixture over the top and scatter with the last of the herbs. Serve immediately.

Trout and cucumber noodles with sushi ginger

Serves 2   *15 minutes preparation: 15 minutes cooking*

Sometimes a dish is made by adding an unexpected ingredient. Here it is the idea of including sushi ginger – those wafer-thin, pink-frilled slices of pickled ginger which always accompany sushi – in a noodle and fish dish. This is a quick and easy after-work dish which is healthy and made with inexpensive, accessible ingredients. Cucumber is terrific in slurping noodle dishes, adding a clean, crisp taste and texture which goes well with the slippery noodles. Here it also looks pretty with the pink fish and snowy-white noodles. I used ready-soaked, pale and chunky udon wheat noodles, but any round (as opposed to flat) rice or wheat noodles would be good. Sushi ginger is sold by health-food shops, some supermarkets and many fishmongers.

½ cucumber
2 spring onions
½ chicken stock cube
3 tbsp soy sauce
150g/5oz udon or any round noodles soaked

6 slices pickled sushi ginger
2 fillets rainbow trout
flour for dusting
1 tbsp vegetable oil

Use a potato peeler to peel the cucumber. Cut it in half lengthways and scrape away the seeds and their watery surround with a teaspoon. Slice into chunky half moons. Trim the spring onions and then finely slice them. Dissolve the stock cube in 300ml/½ pint boiling water. Add the soy sauce, cucumber and spring onions to the stock. Cover and leave for 5 minutes.

At the same time, place the noodles in a separate bowl and cover with boiling water. Leave for 5 minutes. Drain the noodles and divide between two deep bowls. Strain the stock over the top, then stir the cucumber and onions into the noodles. Cut the ginger slices in half and add to the broth.

Halve the trout fillets across the middle. Dust both sides with flour, shaking off the excess. Heat the oil in a frying pan and, when very hot, add the pieces of fish, skin-side down. Fry for a couple of minutes until the skin is crisp, then flip to cook the other side briefly. Lay the fish over the noodles and serve.

Tuna and white bean stew

Serves 4–6 *20 minutes preparation: 40 minutes cooking*

One summer I found myself the happy recipient of a glut of fresh tuna, thanks to a lucky catch by a fisherman friend of the family. I seared it on the griddle and served it with avocado and tomato salsa, I shaved it sushi-style into wafer-thin slices and we ate it with sticky rice and wasabi, and I had another go at my Thai green curry. I was just beginning to wonder what to do next when the latest edition of Australian Gourmet Traveller *popped through my letterbox. Here I found a heart-warming feature on roasts and casseroles and a delicious-sounding recipe for tuna and white bean stew by Jane Hann. Although the list of ingredients makes it sound complicated, I do urge you to give it a go, because it's no trouble to prepare or eat. This is my slightly adjusted version. Serve it with crusty bread to mop up the delicious juices.*

1 onion
1 fennel bulb
2 tbsp olive oil
1 small red chilli
3 canned anchovy fillets
1 large garlic clove
300ml/½ pint chicken or fish stock (a cube is fine)
1 glass white wine, about 150ml/¼ pint

400g/14oz can chopped tomatoes
250g/8oz small potatoes scrubbed
500g/1lb tuna fillet
400g/14oz can cannellini beans
handful coriander or basil leaves
best olive oil to serve
salt and freshly ground black pepper

Peel and finely chop the onion. Trim the root end of the fennel, quarter it lengthways and slice finely. Heat the oil in a spacious, heavy-based saucepan, stir in the onion and fennel, cover the pan and cook over a medium heat for 5 minutes. Give it a stir, season lightly with salt and pepper, return the lid and cook for a further 5 minutes.

Meanwhile, split the chilli, scrape away the seeds and chop finely. Coarsely chop the anchovies. Peel the garlic and chop. Add the chilli, anchovies and garlic to the onion and stir for a couple of minutes. Add the stock and white wine, bring to the boil and simmer for 5 minutes. Now add the tomatoes, bring to the boil again, turn down the heat and cover the pan. Cook for 15–20 minutes until the fennel is tender.

While it is cooking, cook the potatoes in boiling salted water. Drain and keep warm. Cut the tuna into kebab-sized chunks. Tip the beans into a sieve and rinse under cold running water. Add the beans, potatoes and tuna to the stew and cook for 6–8 minutes until the tuna is just cooked through. Stir in the coriander or basil. Serve in warmed bowls with a splash of olive oil.

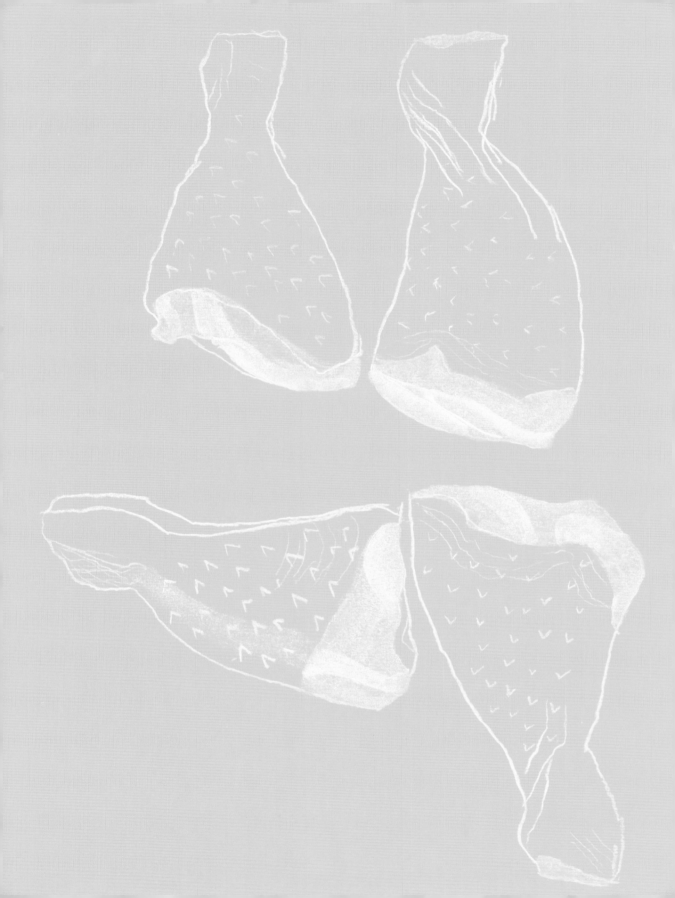

Chicken and duck

Cheat's chicken-and-leek risotto with saffron

Serves 2–3   *20 minutes preparation: 40 minutes cooking*

Most people love risotto but hate the thought of standing over a hot stove for the best part of half-an-hour stirring ladle after ladle of hot stock into the rice. This simple variation on the risotto theme virtually cooks itself and is mindless to make. It isn't made with a risotto rice such as arborio, vialone nano or Spanish carnaroli. Good old basmati makes a terrific risotto-type slop and if the dish is left around to go cold, it becomes the most fabulous filling for a puff-pastry pie. The recipe could also be turned into a soupy meal-in-a-bowl by stirring a dessertspoon of flour into the cooked chicken and dissolving a chicken stock cube in a litre (1¹/₄ pints) water.

1 onion
1 garlic clove
25g/1oz butter
1 tbsp olive oil
1 bay leaf
2 leeks

2 skinless boned chicken thighs
1 small unwaxed lemon
generous pinch saffron dissolved in 1 tbsp hot water
150g/5oz basmati rice
2 tbsp chopped flat leaf parsley
salt and freshly ground black pepper

Peel, halve and finely chop the onion and garlic. Melt the butter with the olive oil in a 2-litre/3½-pint-capacity heavy-based saucepan with a well-fitting lid. Stir in the onion, garlic and bay leaf. Cook, stirring often, for 5 minutes while you trim the leeks and slice into thin rounds. Wash the leeks and shake dry. Stir the leeks into the onion, season generously with salt and pepper, stir again, cover the pan and cook for 5 minutes, stirring once or twice.

Meanwhile, slice the chicken into bite-sized strips. Season the pieces with salt and pepper. Remove the zest from half the lemon, either with a zester or using a potato peeler, cutting small, paper-thin scraps. Stir the chicken, lemon zest and saffron into the vegetables and cook, uncovered, stirring to ensure all the chicken turns from pink to white, for 5 minutes.

Rinse the rice, shake dry and stir it into the pan. Add 350ml/12fl oz water, and juice from half the lemon, bring the liquid to the boil, reduce the heat immediately to very low, cover the pan and cook for 10 minutes. Remove and leave the pan untouched for a further 10 minutes so the rice finishes cooking in the steam. Stir the parsley into the risotto, adjust the seasoning with salt, pepper and lemon juice and serve, risotto-style, in bowls.

Chicken with lemon couscous and black olives

Serves 4   *20 minutes preparation: 15 minutes cooking*

These days, if you want to cut a dash with a quick impromptu supper for friends, the smart ingredient to reach for is couscous. Pasta, useful and delicious though it undoubtedly is, seems passé by comparison. I know, I know, it is ridiculous to compare these two ancient foods, but let me explain that this particular version of couscous was whipped up under testing circumstances. I was visiting a friend who lives part of the year in an isolated cottage. He has no running water and cooks with a single burner which has about as much power as a fading blow torch. Despite the obvious handicaps for this metropolitan cook, the dish was a huge hit, as much for its originality as for the ease with which it was made. It goes spectacularly well with chunks of cucumber in natural yoghurt beaten with crushed garlic, a splash of lemon juice and olive oil.

25g/1oz sultanas
4 large chicken breast fillets
2 lemons (1 for juice, 1 for wedges)
4 tbsp olive oil
2 garlic cloves
25g/1oz pine kernels
pinch saffron

1 chicken stock cube dissolved in 450ml/¾ pint
   boiling water
200g/7oz couscous
25g/1oz pitted black olives
few sprigs coriander
salt

Place the sultanas in a cup and just cover with boiling water. Leave to plump. Slice the chicken into 5cm/2in strips, approximately 1cm/½ in thick. Put the chicken in a shallow dish and squeeze over the juice from half a lemon. Add 1 tablespoon of the olive oil. Peel the garlic, chop finely, sprinkle with a little salt and then crush to a paste. Add the paste to the bowl and mix everything thoroughly. Leave for at least 10 minutes and up to 2 hours.

Heat ½ tablespoon of the olive oil in a frying pan placed over a medium heat and stir-fry the pine kernels for a couple of minutes until lightly golden. Tip onto absorbent kitchen paper to drain. Stir the saffron into the chicken stock. Pour the couscous into a bowl, stir in the stock, the juice from the remaining lemon half and 1 tablespoon of the olive oil. Season with salt and pepper, stir, cover and leave for the couscous to hydrate. Check after 10 minutes: it should be slightly more moist than the usual bone dry. Fork up the couscous, stir in the sultanas and pine kernels and spoon onto a platter. Tear the olives in half and scatter over the top.

Add the last of the oil to the frying pan placed over a high heat. Cook the chicken in batches to encourage fast, even cooking. Allow about 30 seconds a side until golden. Arrange the chicken over the couscous as each batch is ready. Decorate with sprigs of coriander and lemon wedges. Eat hot, warm or cold.

Chicken pilaf

Serves 4   *20 minutes preparation: 40 minutes cooking*

Here's a fantastic way of using the remains of a roast chicken or a small amount of cooked chicken to feed four. Modest ingredients are enlivened with a hint of cinnamon and saffron to become an unbelievably luscious and extremely more-ish dish. For a change, you could also serve the pilaf on a platter garnished with a couple of sliced, hard-boiled eggs to create a beautiful Indian-style biryani. If you have all the necessary ingredients to hand except saffron, the pilaf will still be delicious. A generous pinch of turmeric will colour the rice similarly, but you will miss out on the beguiling saffron flavour and aroma.

2 large onions
1 tbsp olive oil
50g/2oz blanched almonds
50g/2oz butter
1 chicken stock cube
225g/7½oz basmati rice
250g/8oz cooked chicken

handful broken vermicelli or fine thread
    egg noodles
50g/2oz raisins
½ tsp ground cinnamon
generous pinch saffron
salt and freshly ground black pepper
1 lemon, cut into wedges

Peel and halve the onions. Keeping separate piles, thinly slice one half and finely chop the rest. Heat the olive oil in a medium-sized saucepan and, when very hot, stir in the sliced onion. Adjust the heat so the onion sizzles without burning and cook for several minutes until nicely browned and shrivelled. Add the almonds and cook for another minute or so until they take on a bit of colour. Tip the mixture onto absorbent kitchen paper to drain. Wipe out the pan and add the butter. As soon as it is melted, stir in the chopped onion, and cook for about 15 minutes, stirring often, until soft and golden.

Meanwhile, prepare everything else. Wash the rice until the water runs clear. Dissolve the stock cube in 750ml/1½ pints boiling water. Tear the chicken into bite-sized pieces and season generously with salt and pepper. When the onions are ready, stir the vermicelli or noodles into the onions and cook for a couple of minutes until golden. Now add the raisins and cook for a further minute or two before adding the cinnamon and rice. Dissolve the saffron in 2 tablespoons water and add that too. Stir well and cook for 2 more minutes before adding the hot stock. Bring the liquid to the boil, reduce the heat to very low, cover the pan and cook for 10 minutes.

Turn off the heat and leave without removing the lid for a further 10 minutes. Stir the chicken into the pilaf and pile into a serving bowl. Garnish with the browned onion and almonds. Serve with lemon wedges to squeeze over the rice. The pilaf is delicious hot, warm, or cold, although it does turn stodgy as it cools.

Chicken with coriander and tomatoes

Serves 4   *35 minutes preparation: 35 minutes cooking*

A hint of tamarind complements the lemony tang of fresh coriander in this wonderfully rustic chicken and tomato stew. It is easy to make and everybody always seems to like it. The pieces of chicken end up imbued with a fresh tomato sauce, which is thickened with red onions and freshened up with the last-minute addition of masses of chopped coriander leaves, garlic and a little mint. This dish was inspired by something similar I once ate in Portugal. It goes with just about everything, from boiled potatoes, to pasta, rice or a chunk of bread.

750g/1½lb skinned lean chicken pieces
3 tbsp olive oil
3 red onions
large knob butter
750g/1½lb ripe tomatoes
1 bay leaf

1 tbsp tamarind paste
3 garlic cloves, preferably new season
1 large bunch coriander, about 75g/3oz
1 small bunch mint, about 50g/2oz
salt and freshly ground black pepper

Slice the chicken into thick strips, cutting across the grain. Heat 2 tablespoons of the oil in a saucepan that can accommodate all the ingredients. When the oil is very hot, fry the pieces of chicken in batches, cooking for a couple of minutes a side without moving, then turning as the chicken browns and turns crusty. Remove the chicken from the pan.

Meanwhile, peel and halve the onions and slice down the halves to make chunky wedges. When the chicken is all done, add the butter and, as soon as it has sizzled, stir in the onions. Cook briskly, stirring every now and again, until the onions are wilted and scorched in places. While the onions are cooking, place the tomatoes in a bowl and cover with boiling water. Count to 20, drain, peel and chop. Stir the tamarind, bay leaf and tomatoes into the onions. Cook for 10–15 minutes until the tomatoes have broken down a bit, then return the chicken to the pan.

Cook at a steady simmer for about 20 minutes until the chicken is tender. Taste and adjust the seasoning with salt and pepper. Peel the garlic and chop very finely. Coarsely chop the leaves from the bunches of coriander and mint. When the chicken is done and the tomatoes and onions have made a thick, chunky sauce, stir in the chopped herbs and the finely chopped garlic and serve.

Chicken with lentils and bacon

Serves 4–5   *20 minutes preparation: 25 minutes cooking*

A comforting, stewy dish that takes no time to cook and instantly fills the kitchen with delicious homely smells. Most ingredients are fresh and their choice and the way they are prepared are crucial to the speed of the dish. Leftovers reheat perfectly.

2 red onions
2 large garlic cloves
25g/1oz butter
1 tbsp cooking oil
2 celery sticks
2 carrots
1 bay leaf
450g/14½oz skinless boned chicken

½ tsp thyme leaves
6 medium tomatoes, about 500g/1lb
400g/14oz can green lentils
squeeze lemon juice
100g/3½oz bacon
1 tbsp coarsely chopped flat leaf parsley
100g/3½oz frozen peas
salt and freshly ground black pepper

Peel, halve and slice the onions. Peel and coarsely chop the garlic. Melt half the butter with half the cooking oil in a spacious saucepan over a medium heat. Add the onion and garlic, season generously with salt and pepper and cook until the onion is wilted and juicy.

Meanwhile, trim the celery and carrots and peel both with a potato peeler. Finely slice the celery and grate the carrots. Add both, and the bay leaf, to the onion, season again with salt and pepper and cook, stirring a few times, for 5 minutes. While the vegetable are cooking, slice the chicken across the grain into 3.5 x 1cm/1½ x ½in strips. Sprinkle it with the thyme.

Place the tomatoes in a bowl and cover with boiling water. Count to 20, drain and use a small knife to cut the cores out in a cone shape and remove the skin. Tip the lentils into a sieve and rinse with cold water. Shake dry.

Add the chicken to the vegetables with the remaining butter and oil, and stir around as the chicken plumps and turns white all over. Now add the tomatoes, crushing them down into the pan to break them up. Squeeze over the lemon juice and continue cooking until the tomatoes have flopped to make a juicy sauce. This takes 10–15 minutes. While it is cooking, slice across the bacon rashers to make little sticks. Heat a small frying pan and fry the bacon until it is very crisp. Tip onto absorbent kitchen paper to drain.

When the sauce is ready, add the prepared lentils and frozen peas. Simmer for a couple of minutes to heat the lentils and cook the peas through, taste and adjust the seasoning with salt and pepper. Serve with a garnish of parsley and crisp bacon bits.

Chicken and cashew nut noodle stir-fry

Serves 2   *15 minutes preparation: 10 minutes cooking*

The shops are awash with stir-fry sauces and every condiment needed for authentic and ersatz Chinese food, but this simple stir-fry requires nothing more than soy sauce and sherry to give the dish a recognizable Chinese flavour. Marinating the chicken in a mixture of egg white, cornflour and salt has the double effect of softening the texture of the meat and providing a thin, light batter. As always with stir-fries, the important point is to get all the slicing done before you start cooking and to line up the ingredients so they are quick and easy to fling into the wok. Rice noodles have become familiar through Thai cooking and the ones you want have various names but look like thin, off-white tagliatelle and are folded like a skein of wool before they are stuffed into their cellophane packets. They don't need to be cooked and just require a few minutes soaking in boiling water before they turn snowy white. The quantities given provide plenty for two greedy portions, but leftovers are delicious cold – perfect, I'd say, for tomorrow's lunch box.

2 chicken breast fillets
1 egg white
2 tsp cornflour
75g/3oz flat rice noodles
25g/1oz piece fresh ginger
125g/4oz bunch spring onions

2 tbsp soy sauce (I use Kikkoman)
2 tbsp dry sherry
small bunch chives (optional)
3 tbsp vegetable oil
50g/2oz cashew nuts
salt

Slice the chicken into thin, bite-sized strips. Whisk the egg white with the cornflour and ½ teaspoon salt until fluffy, white and smooth. Immerse the chicken in the mixture and chill in the fridge while you prepare everything else. Place the noodles in a pan or bowl and cover with boiling water. Cover and leave for at least 4 minutes to soften. Drain them just before you begin to cook.

Peel the ginger and slice into matchsticks. Trim the spring onions and slice into skinny strips the length of your little finger. Measure out the soy and sherry. Snip the chives, if using.

Heat the wok over a high flame. Add 2 tablespoons of the oil and swirl it round the wok. Add the chicken and quickly spread it out, turning it almost immediately and adjusting the heat so it forms a thin crust that doesn't blacken. Once all the meat has turned white and is patched with golden brown – after about 1 minute – tip it onto a plate.

Wipe out the wok, add the rest of the oil and stir-fry the cashew nuts, ginger and spring onions for a minute or so until the onions wilt. Add the soy mixture and return the chicken. Stir-fry for another 30 seconds, add the noodles and mix. Remove from the heat, stir in the chives, if using, and tip into bowls. Eat with chopsticks or a fork.

Chicken tom yam

Serves 4   *20 minutes preparation: 30 minutes cooking*

*This is a great soup if you're feeling a bit jaded. One whiff clears the sinuses and brings tears to the eyes. Its golden broth is an unholy balance of hot and sour from chillies, lime juice and salty Thai fish sauce with a complementary undercurrent of lemon grass and ginger. This addictive liquid is good enough to drink as a tonic, although it is quickly turned into a delicious healthy, low-fat soup with even more layers of flavour. It's most often made with prawns (*tom yam kung*), occasionally with white fish or squid, and is sometimes on restaurant menus as a vegetarian option with tofu and mushrooms. My meal-in-a-bowl version is a slightly more elaborate mixture of flavours and textures than is usual. Although this soup is at its most superior when made with fresh chicken stock, it's still worth making with stock cubes.*

3 lemon grass stalks	50g/2oz green beans
25g/1oz piece fresh ginger	4 spring onions
4 small green chillies	1 tbsp coriander leaves
1.5 litres/2½ pints chicken stock	3 limes (2 for juice, 1 for wedges)
4 large skinless boneless chicken thighs	2 tbsp Thai fish sauce (*nam pla*)
150g/5oz button mushrooms	salt

Smash the lemon grass stalks with something heavy to split them. Peel and finely slice the ginger, cutting it into matchsticks. Place the lemon grass, ginger, chillies and ½ teaspoon salt in a saucepan with the stock. Bring to the boil, reduce the heat, cover the pan and simmer for 15 minutes.

Meanwhile, cut the chicken into bite-sized chunks. Wipe, then halve or quarter the mushrooms. Top and tail the beans and slice into small pieces. Finely slice the spring onions. Coarsely chop the coriander. Fish the lemon grass out of the stock and, if you are a chilli freak, finely slice the chillies and return. If not, remove them.

Stir the juice from 2 of the limes and the fish sauce into the pot, then add chicken and mushrooms. Cook gently for 10 minutes without boiling. Add the beans and spring onions. Cook for a further couple of minutes, stir in the coriander leaves and serve with a wedge of lime.

Chicken and shrimp gumbo

Serves 4   *20 minutes preparation: 30 minutes cooking*

In Louisiana the dish everyone loves and has a view about is gumbo. Some people guard their family recipes as if they were the key to heaven, but this hearty Creole or Cajun meal-in-a-bowl is always hot enough to remind you that this is Tabasco country. My quick, after-work version doesn't fall into the usual gumbo categories in that it isn't thickened with okra or filé, a powder made from dried young sassafras leaves which originally came from the Choctaw Indians. Gumbo always includes the famous Creole trinity of celery, onion and green pepper and this one is coloured as well as thickened with paprika. Any mild paprika would be fine, but I particularly recommend 'soft' smoked paprika if you can find it. Serve as a soup or spoon it over boiled rice.

1 large celery heart	½ tsp thyme
1 green pepper	1 chicken stock cube
1 onion	1 tsp 'soft' smoked paprika
2 garlic cloves	½ tbsp flour
1 leek	3 tsp Tabasco sauce
2 fresh or canned peeled tomatoes	generous handful flat leaf parsley leaves
4 large skinless boneless chicken thighs	about 250g/8oz cooked peeled prawns
4 tbsp cooking oil	squeeze lemon or lime juice
1 bay leaf	salt

Finely slice the celery. Wash and shake dry. Dice the pepper, discarding the seeds and white membrane. Peel, halve and finely chop the onion. Peel and thinly slice the garlic. Trim and split the leek and slice thinly. Chop the tomatoes. Slice the chicken into bite-sized chunks.

Heat 1 tablespoon of the oil in a spacious heavy-based saucepan and quickly brown the chicken in batches, transferring it to a plate as you go. Heat the remaining oil in the pan and stir in the onion, pepper, celery, garlic, bay leaf and thyme. Cook briskly, stirring often, for about 10 minutes until the vegetables are juicy and beginning to soften but not brown. Add the leek and cook for a couple of minutes.

Dissolve the stock cube in 600ml/1 pint hot water. Sprinkle the paprika and flour over the vegetables, stir well and cook for a minute before adding the chicken, stock and Tabasco. Bring to the boil, immediately turn down the heat and simmer for 10 minutes.

Meanwhile, coarsely chop the parsley. Add the parsley, prawns and tomato to the pan. Reheat, taste and adjust the seasoning with salt and lemon or lime juice. Serve immediately or reheat as required, adding extra parsley for colour.

Chinese noodle salad

Serves 3–4   *20 minutes preparation: 20 minutes cooking*

Cucumber is the novelty in this delicious dish, inspired by something I once ate at Mr Kai in Mayfair, London. The cucumber strips soften slightly in the noodle heat, but the joy of this dish is the contrast of textures as well as the deliciously subtle flavours. It's the perfect fridge standby and ideal for lunch boxes because it's a complete meal that is satisfying and relatively healthy.

½ chicken stock cube
25g/1oz piece fresh ginger, sliced
2–4 garlic cloves, crushed (optional)
4 spring onions
4 large chicken thighs or 2 legs
1 red chilli

½ cucumber
150g/5oz fine thread egg noodles
1 tbsp cider vinegar
1 tbsp toasted sesame oil
squeeze lemon juice
salt

Place the stock cube, 600ml/1 pint water, most of the sliced ginger, the crushed garlic clove and spring onion greens in a medium-sized saucepan. Season lightly with salt and bring to the boil. Trim away any excess fat and skin from the chicken thighs or, if using legs, joint them with a sharp knife. Add the chicken to the boiling stock, return the liquid to the boil and immediately turn the heat to low. Cover the pan and simmer for 15 minutes.

Meanwhile, finely slice the white of the spring onions. Split the chilli, scrape away the seeds and slice into skinny batons and then into tiny dice. Cut the remaining ginger into tiny dice. Split the cucumber in half lengthways. Use a teaspoon to scrape out the seeds and their watery surrounds. Halve the cucumber across the width. Slice each half lengthways into very thin ribbons, each with a share of dark green skin.

Check that the chicken is cooked through and lift out of the pan onto a chopping board. Scoop the ginger slices and spring onion greens out of the pan (leave the garlic) and add the noodles. Increase the heat to boil the stock, tossing the noodles to disentangle and keep submerged. Reduce the heat slightly and boil gently for 3 minutes until most of the stock has been absorbed. Cover the pan and turn off the heat, but keep covered for a minute or so until the stock is completely absorbed, leaving the noodles glossy.

Tip the noodles into a serving bowl. Add the vinegar and sesame oil and toss thoroughly. Discard the chicken skin and use a fork and sharp knife to shred the chicken meat. Add it and all the other ingredients and toss well. Season with lemon juice, toss again and serve.

Cock-a-leekie

Serves 2–3   *15 minutes preparation: 40 minutes cooking*

This adaptation of the famous Scottish soup makes a wonderful, comforting supper. Not only does the dish look interesting – black prunes against white chicken and verdant leek greens – but it is also a surprisingly good mix of textures and flavours. It is particularly delicious with brown bread and butter and a nip of whisky.

4 skinless chicken thighs
large bunch flat leaf parsley, about 75g/3oz
1 bay leaf
3 sprigs thyme
2 garlic cloves

3 medium leeks, about 175g/6oz
1 small onion
10 prunes
100g/3½oz basmati rice
salt and freshly ground black pepper

Place the chicken thighs in a medium-sized saucepan with 750ml/1½ pints water. Bring slowly to the boil. Remove the grey scum that forms. Meanwhile, pick the leaves off the parsley and set aside. Bundle the parsley stalks, bay leaf and thyme together with cotton or string. Crush the garlic cloves and flake away the skin. Trim the leeks and slice the white part into 2.5cm/1in rounds. Peel, halve and thinly slice the onion. Add the herb bundle, garlic, leeks and onion to the pan. Add ½ teaspoon salt and plenty of black pepper. Return to the boil, reduce the heat and simmer gently for 15 minutes.

Meanwhile, finely slice the leek greens, discarding only the very fibrous ends. Rinse and shake dry. If necessary, remove the stones from the prunes. Coarsely chop the parsley leaves: you want about 3 tablespoons. Discard the herb bundle and add the rice to the pan, letting it trickle under the leeks (which will float on top). Return to the boil, reduce the heat immediately and simmer for 15 minutes. Five minutes before the end of cooking add the prunes, poking them among the now plump rice. Add the leek greens and half the parsley. Simmer briskly for 3 minutes – the leek greens should remain *al dente*.

Leave to rest for a couple of minutes, then stir in the remaining parsley. Taste and adjust the seasoning. For ease of eating, and to make the chicken go further, cut the meat off the bones before you serve. This is best done before the leek greens are added.

Sweetcorn and grilled red pepper chicken chowder

Serves 4   *25 minutes preparation: 35 minutes cooking*

The time to make this soup is towards the end of the summer when corn-on-the-cob and sweet red peppers are dirt cheap and the local fruit and veg stall is virtually giving them away. The slight crunch of the fresh sweetcorn goes very well with the soft chunks of poached chicken, the slippery pieces of grilled red pepper and strands of onion. Everything is livened up with the occasional sting of chilli and curious charm of fresh coriander. Grilling the peppers, incidentally, does not just make them easy to peel. Grilling, like roasting, noticeably concentrates their flavour and means they will be almost cooked when they join the other ingredients in the pan.

2 red peppers	2 corn-on-the-cob
1 red onion	500g/1lb boneless chicken
25g/1oz butter	large bunch coriander, about 75g/3oz
1 tbsp cooking oil	1 chicken stock cube dissolved in 500ml/17fl oz
1 plump garlic clove	boiling water
1 small red chilli	salt and freshly ground black pepper

Pre-heat the overhead grill to its highest setting. Lay the red peppers out on the grill pan. Place it close to the hot grill and cook the peppers, turning every few minutes, until their skin is blistered and blackened all over. Place the peppers in a sealed plastic bag or in a bowl covered with clingfilm. Leave for about 10 minutes to sweat and 'lift' the skin. Peel away the charred skin. Quarter the peppers lengthways, discard the stalk, white seeds and membrane and chop into pieces the size of a postage stamp.

Meanwhile, peel the onion, halve and finely slice into half moons. Place a saucepan that can hold the entire dish over a medium heat. Add the butter and cooking oil and, when the butter has melted, stir in the onion. Let it soften without colouring, allowing at least 10 minutes, probably 15. While the onion is cooking, peel and finely chop the garlic. Split the chilli, use a teaspoon to scrape away the seeds and chop very finely. Remove the cob leaves and 'silk' if necessary. Trim the end of the cob, stand upright and use a large, sharp knife to slice the kernels off the cob. Discard the cob.

Slice the chicken into kebab-sized chunks. Coarsely chop the bunch of coriander, stalks included, setting aside 2 tablespoons leaves. When the onion is ready, stir in the garlic and chilli. Cook until the garlic is aromatic – not long – then stir in the corn kernels. Cover the pan, reduce the heat slightly and cook, stirring a couple of times, for 10 minutes.

Add the chicken, tossing it around until it is all white. Add most of the coriander and the diced red pepper. Season generously with salt and pepper. Add the stock. Bring to the boil, reduce the heat immediately and simmer for 5–10 minutes until the chicken is tender. Taste and adjust the seasoning with salt and pepper. Add the remaining coriander, stir and serve.

Japanese chicken in a bowl with ponzu

Serves 4   *20 minutes preparation: 15 minutes cooking*

If you can imagine minestrone with a pungent sour sauce instead of the pesto-style sharpener that lifts this chunky soup, then you are well on the way to understanding this recipe. It is the mix of textures as well as flavours that makes this meal-in-a-bowl. If you are lucky enough to have some home-made stock, now is the time to use it. The great thing about this dish is that the chicken and vegetables contribute to the flavour of the broth as they cook. Although I have made this with chicken, it could be made with a firm-textured fish such as monkfish or hoki, or with tofu if you are a vegetarian. The soup is delicious enough on its own but the salty, citrus ponzu *liquor gives it an incredible lift. Any rice noodles or just-soak Japanese noodles such as soba or medium egg noodles, are perfect for this dish. I used the ones that look like tagliatelle and their softness added bulk without interfering with texture or flavour. Mirin, a sweet, distilled rice wine, and rice vinegar are available in most supermarkets and health shops.*

150g/5oz rice noodles
1 litre/1¾ pints chicken stock or 2 stock cubes
    dissolved in 1 litre/1¾ pints hot water
4 large skinless boneless chicken thighs
1 carrot, about 100g/3½oz
125g/4oz shiitake mushrooms
1 leek
½ cucumber

125g/4oz mangetout or sugar snap peas
100g/3½oz spinach
3 tbsp mirin
1 lemon
1 lime
3 tbsp dark soy sauce
3 tbsp rice vinegar

Generously cover the noodles with boiling water, cover and leave to soften. Bring the stock to the boil in a large pan. Cut the chicken into bite-sized chunks and add to the stock. Return to boiling, then adjust the heat so the liquid simmers. Cook the chicken for 6 minutes.

Meanwhile, keeping everything in separate piles, peel and slice the carrot. Wipe and slice the mushrooms. Trim the leek and slice in thin rounds. Peel the cucumber, halve it lengthways and use a teaspoon to scrape out the seeds and watery surround, then slice in chunky half moons. Halve the mangetout or sugar snap peas lengthways. Shred the spinach.

Add the carrot to the chicken. Cook for 2 minutes, then add the mushrooms. Cook for 2 more minutes and add the leek. Now add the cucumber and, 2 minutes later, the mangetout. Drain the noodles and add them. Stir in the spinach and turn off the heat.

Make the *ponzu* by pouring the mirin into a small saucepan. Quickly bring to the boil and boil for 10 seconds. Pour it into a bowl, add the juice from the lemon and lime, the soy sauce and vinegar. Mix thoroughly. Serve the soup with chopsticks and a spoon and a bowl of *ponzu* for dunking the big chunks and seasoning the soup.

Magenta chicken curry

Serves 4   *20 minutes preparation: 55 minutes cooking*

Now that beetroot has been claimed as a health food which can do wonders for your love-life, I've been trying out a few alternatives to the British salad staple of beetroot in vinegar. When grated and boiled in water, it produces the most exquisitely vibrant purple liquid, which has the power to turn pale food into magenta-coloured masterpieces. It brings a new vivacity to curries and is a new take on your average 'ruby' (Cockney rhyming slang for a curry). This chicken curry looks spectacular served with a scoop of white yoghurt, and has a deliciously intriguing flavour that is all at once hot, sweet and sour. Serve it in a warmed tortilla with yoghurt and a few sprigs of coriander or over rice with yoghurt or raita, mango chutney and poppadoms.

1 dried red chilli	1 tbsp ground coriander
1 onion	200g/7oz Greek-style natural yoghurt
3 tbsp vegetable oil	2 raw beetroot
3 plump garlic cloves	1 small lemon
50g/2oz piece fresh ginger	salt
750g/1½lb boneless chicken	

Place the chilli in a cup and just cover with boiling water. Leave to soak while you peel and finely chop the onion. Heat the oil in a large frying pan or similarly wide-based saucepan placed over a medium-low heat. Add the onion and fry, stirring occasionally, for 6–7 minutes until soft and golden.

Meanwhile, peel and finely chop the garlic. Peel the ginger and slice thinly into small scraps. Cut the chicken into bite-sized pieces. Remove the chilli from its soaking water. Split it lengthways, scrape away the seeds and chop into tiny pieces. Stir the garlic, ginger and chilli into the softened onion and cook for a further 3–4 minutes. Add the ground coriander and fry for a further 30 seconds. Increase the heat slightly, add the chicken to the pan and stir-fry for 5 or 6 minutes until all the pieces have turned from pink to white. Season the chicken with ½ teaspoon salt and stir in the yoghurt. Reduce the heat to low, cover the pan – use a double fold of foil if your pan doesn't have a lid – and cook for 15 minutes.

Meanwhile, use a potato peeler to peel the beetroot and grate them on the large hole of a cheese grater directly into a small saucepan. Add 300ml/½ pint water and the juice of half the lemon and cook, partially covered, for 10–15 minutes until the beetroot is tender. Tip the beetroot and water into the chicken. Stir thoroughly and cook, uncovered, for a further 5–10 minutes until the curry is thick and all the flavours amalgamated. Taste and adjust the seasoning with salt and lemon juice. This curry reheats perfectly.

Rosemary and lemon chicken big soup

Serves 4   *20 minutes preparation: 45 minutes cooking*

Big in flavour and big in satisfaction is the name of the game with this chunky soup. It is virtually a store-cupboard supper, relying for freshness on easily available ingredients. It's the sort of meal-in-a-bowl that requires very little cooking and simmers away on the back burner giving out wonderfully heartening smells as you potter around doing other things. Should there be leftovers, they will reheat perfectly, although you will probably need to add extra liquid – water will do – because the lentils will go on drinking in the juices.

1 large unwaxed lemon
about 250g/8oz lean chicken thigh meat
1 large red onion
3 large garlic cloves
2 tbsp olive oil
1 tbsp rosemary leaves
1 bay leaf
150g/5oz Puy lentils

1 large flat mushroom
150g/5oz carrots
400g/14oz can chopped tomatoes
1 chicken stock cube dissolved in 600ml/1 pint
   boiling water
small bunch flat leaf parsley
salt and freshly ground black pepper

Remove the zest from the lemon and cut it into small scraps. Squeeze the juice from half the lemon into a bowl. Finely slice the chicken into short ribbons and fold it into the lemon juice.

Peel the onion and quarter it lengthways. Slice thinly across the quarters. Peel the garlic and slice in thin rounds. Heat the oil over a medium-high heat and stir in the onion and garlic. Cook, stirring often, for 5 minutes, then add the lemon zest. Finely chop the rosemary and add that too, together with the bay leaf. Reduce the heat and stir in the lentils. Wipe the mushroom and chop into chunky dice. Add it to the pan. Peel and chop the carrots and add them too. Cook, stirring constantly, for about 5 more minutes, then add the tomatoes. Let the juices bubble up and add the stock. Bring to the boil and reduce the heat. Three-quarters cover the pan and simmer for 30 minutes.

Add 1 teaspoon salt, plenty of pepper, the chicken and the juice from the remaining lemon half. Increase the heat, stir well and, as soon as you see bubbles forming round the edge, turn off the heat, cover the pan and leave for 5 minutes. Taste and adjust the seasoning. Stir in the parsley and serve.

Pimiento, chickpeas and chicken with chorizo

Serves 4   *20 minutes preparation: 25 minutes cooking*

One of my favourite ingredients, something I always keep alongside my stash of canned tomatoes, is a jar of peeled and roasted Spanish red peppers (pimientos) in olive oil. They cost about four times as much as the tinned equivalent (which aren't roasted and come in brine), but there is no comparison in flavour. They turn an egg or cheese-on-toast supper into a treat and are great in sandwiches (try with mozzarella and avocado). Arranged on a platter as part of a cold spread, they look exceedingly handsome. They are useful, too, in pasta and rice dishes and are quickly blitzed into a delicious sauce, such as I've made for this Spanish-style almost-store-cupboard supper. Serve with crusty bread and muchos rioja.

6 waxy potatoes
1 large red onion, about 200g/7oz
2 plump garlic cloves
275g/9oz roasted red peppers (pimientos) in olive oil
300g/10oz skinless boneless chicken
400g/14oz can chickpeas

150g/5oz sliced chorizo
4 tomatoes (best flavour you can find)
Tabasco sauce
squeeze lemon juice
3 tbsp chopped flat leaf parsley
salt

Boil the potatoes in salted water in a medium-sized heavy-based saucepan until tender. Drain, immerse in cold water for about 30 seconds, peel, chop into chunks and set aside. Meanwhile, peel, halve and slice the onion. Peel and slice the garlic in rounds. Reserve 2 tablespoons olive oil from the roasted pimientos. Heat the oil in the potato pan placed over a medium heat. Stir in the onion and garlic, season with salt and cook for about 10 minutes until the onion is beginning to brown and wilt.

Meanwhile, slice the chicken into strips. Tip the chickpeas into a sieve and rinse with cold water. Brown the chicken with the onion, turning the pieces as they turn white around the edges. Add the chorizo, increase the heat slightly, and stir-fry for a few minutes until the oil begins to run.

Tip the pimientos into the bowl of a food processor. Add the whole tomatoes, a generous shake of Tabasco and a squeeze of lemon juice. Blitz until smooth. Add this sauce to the pan together with the drained chickpeas, potato chunks and most of the parsley. Simmer for 5 minutes, taste and adjust the seasoning with salt, lemon juice and Tabasco if you like it very hot. Scatter over the remaining parsley and serve.

Quick cassoulet

Serves 4   *30 minutes preparation: 60 minutes cooking*

It was talk of what to do with the remains of the Christmas goose that started me off. In the Languedoc, where cassoulet originates, it's a complex, hearty concoction of preserved duck, lamb, pork, sausages and dried butter beans. The stew simmers away for hours and is ready when the meat is meltingly soft and the beans have soaked up all the stock. A crusty topping of breadcrumbs and parsley absorbs any fat and keeps the dish moist. This relatively quick version is made along the same lines. It's extremely tasty and satisfying. Serve with lemon wedges to squeeze over the top and lightly cooked French beans.

1 large onion
3 large garlic cloves
2 tbsp cooking oil
4 rashers rindless streaky bacon
1 bay leaf
½ tsp thyme
1 tsp chopped sage
4 good-quality pork sausages
400g/14oz can peeled tomatoes

½ chicken stock cube dissolved in 300ml/½ pint hot water
4 skinless duck breasts
400g/14oz can cannellini or similar white beans
2 tbsp chopped flat leaf parsley
65g/2½oz stale bread, without crusts
1–2 tbsp olive oil
salt and freshly ground black pepper

Peel, halve and finely slice the onion. Peel and slice 2 of the garlic cloves. Heat 1 tablespoon of the cooking oil in a large, heavy-based saucepan until very hot. Stir in the onion. Cook, stirring often, for 4 minutes. Salt generously, reduce the heat to low, stir in the sliced garlic, cover the pan and leave to cook for 10 minutes.

Slice the bacon across the rashers and add to the pan with the bay leaf, thyme and sage. Increase the heat slightly and quickly brown the sausages. Add the tomatoes, breaking them up in the pan, and the stock. Season lightly with salt and generously with black pepper. Simmer, uncovered, for 15 minutes, so the sausages poach and the liquid thickens and reduces.

Meanwhile, cut each duck breast into four large pieces. Heat the remaining cooking oil in a frying pan and brown the duck. Add the duck and its juices to the saucepan. Rinse the beans and add them too. Establish a gentle simmer. Stir in 1 tablespoon of the parsley and check the seasoning, adjusting as necessary. Blitz the bread and the remaining garlic clove to make crumbs, and stir in the remaining parsley. Spread the breadcrumb mixture over the top of the cassoulet, cover the pan and cook for 30 minutes.

Pre-heat the overhead grill. Remove the pan lid, criss-cross the cassoulet with a thin stream of olive oil and place the pan under the grill. Cook until crusty and golden, but watch like a hawk to avoid burning.

Borscht with chicken

Serves 4   *30 minutes preparation: 50 minutes cooking*

There's no such thing as a definitive recipe for borscht, the famous sweet-sour beetroot soup from the Ukraine. There are many regional variations made with different vegetables apart from the ubiquitous beetroot, some with meat and others with mushrooms. I've even come across a fish version with cucumber instead of the more usual cabbage, carrot and potato. One of the finest recipes requires discarding the vegetables after they've flavoured and clarified the broth to reveal a sparklingly clear magenta soup. In this borscht, the soup is thick with vegetables and the broth is flavoured in the traditional way with beer – if it is flat, so much the better. I've added two chicken legs to enrich the flavours and turn the soup into more of a meal. If you don't eat meat, leave out the chicken and the stock cube which, I think, give the soup a bit more oomph.

1 large onion
2 large garlic cloves
2 tbsp olive oil
1 large raw beetroot, about 325g/11oz, and 1 small
  raw beetroot, about 150g/5oz
375g/12oz waxy potatoes
2 medium carrots
2 free-range chicken legs or 4 large thighs or
  drumsticks

300ml/½ pint beer
½ chicken stock cube
250g/8oz red cabbage
200g/7oz canned chopped tomatoes
2 tbsp balsamic or other good red wine vinegar
1–2 tsp sugar
soured cream
dill or chives
salt and freshly ground black pepper

Peel, halve and finely slice the onion. Peel the garlic and slice very thinly. Heat the oil in a large pan and stir both in. Add salt and cook for about 10 minutes until floppy and golden.

Meanwhile, peel the large beetroot and chop into small dice. Do the same with the potato and carrots. Stir the diced beetroot and potatoes into the onion, cook for a couple of minutes, then add the carrots and chicken. Pour on the beer and 1 litre/1¾ pints cold water and crumble in the stock cube. Bring the soup to the boil – this takes several minutes – and adjust the heat so it simmers steadily when three-quarters covered with a lid. Cook for 15 minutes.

Meanwhile, quarter and core the cabbage and slice as thinly as possible. Add to the soup with the tomatoes, vinegar and a generous pinch of salt. Stir well, increase the heat and return to the boil. Adjust the heat again as before, cover as before and cook for a further 15 minutes or until all the vegetables are tender. Taste the broth and adjust and balance the seasoning with salt, pepper, sugar and possibly a dash more vinegar. Peel the small beetroot and grate it directly into the soup to inject deep colour and fresh flavour. Cook for a further 5–10 minutes.

Remove the chicken and flake the meat off the bones into the soup (or garnish individual servings). Serve the soup immediately or, better still, allow to sit, covered, for up to 30 minutes before serving with a blob of soured cream and a final garnish of snipped herbs.

Moroccan chicken, egg and almond tagine

Serves 2   *20 minutes preparation: 35 minutes cooking*

The tagines of Morocco are perfect dishes to serve at any time of the year, whatever the weather. This one is a new, after-work favourite and transforms chicken fillets into something really interesting and satisfying. If you want to make the dish for four people, just double up on the ingredients. If you don't like garlic – though the resultant flavour is very subtle, contributing to the overall interest of the dish – then leave it out. The perfect accompaniment is couscous. For two generous portions, you will need 100g/3½oz couscous hydrated in 250ml/8fl oz boiling water. A splash of olive oil or a knob of butter with a squeeze of lemon makes it more interesting.

2 large onions, about 300g/10oz in total
3 tbsp olive oil
25g/1oz butter
½ tsp ground cumin
½ tsp ground coriander
generous pinch saffron
2 boneless chicken breasts

1 large garlic clove
2 eggs, hard-boiled
½ tbsp vegetable oil
25g/1oz blanched almonds
large bunch fresh coriander
1 lemon or lime (for wedges)
salt and freshly ground black pepper

Peel and halve the onions. Slice one very thinly and finely chop the other. Heat 2 tablespoons of the olive oil and the butter in a 2-litre/3½-pint-capacity, heavy-based pan placed over a medium heat. When the butter has melted, stir in the onions. Fry for 5 minutes, then stir in the cumin and ground coriander and a generous seasoning of salt and pepper. Soften the saffron in 1 tablespoon boiling water and add that too. Reduce the heat, cover the pan and cook for 15 minutes.

Meanwhile, slice the chicken into bite-sized strips. Peel and finely chop the garlic. Sprinkle it with ½ teaspoon salt and use a pestle and mortar or the flat of a knife to work to a juicy paste. Stir the remaining olive oil into the garlic and smear it all over the chicken. Peel and quarter the eggs. Heat the vegetable oil in a second frying pan and stir-fry the almonds for a couple of minutes until evenly golden. Tip on to absorbent kitchen paper to drain.

When the onions are ready, stir in the chicken and cook, stirring frequently, for a couple of minutes until all the pieces have turned white. Add just enough water to cover, bring to the boil, reduce the heat, cover and cook for 15 minutes. Chop the coriander leaves, stir into the tagine together with the almonds and cook for a couple more minutes. Taste and adjust the seasoning. Serve garnished with the hard-boiled eggs and a lemon or lime wedge on the side.

Duck noodles with ginger

Serves 2   *15 minutes preparation: 15–20 minutes cooking*

Slurpy noodle dishes are perfect quick, after-work suppers. All the supermarkets now sell a wide range of cooked noodles, ready to be slipped into a highly seasoned broth or piled into a wok for an impromptu stir-fry. Cooking your own noodles from scratch works out far cheaper than those ready-cooked packs and if you cook double the quantity you need, toss them with a little oil and stash the cooled noodles in a plastic bag or box in the fridge; they'll keep for a few days in perfect condition. This is one of those quick-and-easy noodle meal-in-a-bowl suppers for two that makes the most of ordinary, seasonal vegetables and one meaty duck fillet. A splash of soy sauce added to the broth and a generous seasoning of ginger and garlic add up to a very tasty and texturally interesting dish that is both satisfying and healthy.

150g/5oz dried egg noodles
1 leek or bunch spring onions
1 carrot
25g/1oz piece fresh ginger
1 plump garlic clove
1 duck breast fillet

1 chicken stock cube
1 tbsp soy sauce
1 tbsp groundnut oil
1 tbsp coarsely chopped coriander
salt

Bring a large saucepan of water to the boil. Add the noodles and salt generously. Return to the boil and boil hard for 2 minutes. Drain, return to the pan and cover to keep warm.

Meanwhile, trim the leek and slice thinly on the slant. If using spring onions, trim and slice in long, thin, diagonal slices. In both cases include the green part that isn't tough and coarse. Peel the carrot and slice thinly on the slant. Peel the ginger and slice thinly, cutting it into small pieces. Peel the garlic and slice into paper-thin rounds.

Slice across the duck fillet, cutting it into bite-sized, thin strips. Dissolve the stock cube in 500ml/17fl oz boiling water. Stir in the soy sauce. Heat a wok or frying pan and, when very hot and beginning to smoke, add the oil, swirling it round the pan, followed by the leek, carrot, garlic and ginger. Stir-fry for 5 minutes, keeping everything on the move so nothing burns, then add the duck.

Cook for a further couple of minutes until the meat has all changed colour. Add the stock and bring to the boil, reduce the heat immediately and simmer for 10 minutes. Add the drained noodles, stir well and simmer for a couple of minutes to heat through. Spoon into two suitable bowls, garnish with the coriander and eat with a fork and spoon.

Thai green duck curry with coriander noodles

Serves 4   *15 minutes preparation: 35 minutes cooking*

Twenty years ago very few people without the benefit of a Thai holiday would have come across satay, pad Thai or green curry, or knew the meaning of sambal or would be familiar with the addictive flavours of lemon grass and fresh coriander. Today we can't get enough Thai food, with its exotic flavours, fiery-hot curries and coconut-milk gravies. The predominance of lightly cooked vegetables and seafood, and minimal use of meat, make it very much a cuisine of our times. The fresh pineapple is a delicious contrast which counteracts the chilli heat beautifully.

2 skinless Barbary duck fillets, about 500g/1lb
1 garlic clove
3 shallots or 6 pink Thai shallots
100g/3½oz fine French beans
225g/7½oz can sliced bamboo shoots in water
1 red chilli
5cm/2in slice fresh pineapple, about 250g/8oz
1 tbsp vegetable oil

2 tbsp Thai green curry paste
400ml/14fl oz can coconut milk
1 lemon grass stalk
1 tbsp Thai fish sauce (*nam pla*)
1 lime
large handful coarsely chopped coriander
200g/7oz rice sticks (tagliatelle-width rice noodles)
knob of butter

Get everything ready and assembled before you start cooking. Slice the duck across the grain into 5 x 1cm/2 x ½in strips. Peel and chop the garlic and shallots. Trim the French beans and halve. Rinse and drain the bamboo shoots. Trim the chilli, split lengthways, scrape away the seeds and slice into long, thin strips. Chop into tiny dice. Remove the skin from the pineapple and cut into chunks, discarding the woody central core.

Heat a wok, large frying pan or 2-litre/3½-pint-capacity saucepan and add the oil, curry paste and 3 tablespoons of the coconut milk. Stir-fry for a couple of minutes, then add the garlic and shallots. Toss for another couple of minutes and add the meat, cooking for a few minutes until coloured on all sides. Give the lemon grass a bash with a rolling pin to release its flavour and add that too, together with the fish sauce and remaining coconut milk.

Adjust the heat and leave to simmer, stirring occasionally, for 25 minutes or until the duck is tender. Taste and adjust the seasoning with lime juice. Do not worry if the gravy seems very chilli-hot. When the duck is tender, stir in the bamboo shoots, half the coriander and the pineapple. Heat through before transferring to a warmed bowl. Cover to keep warm. Cook the beans for 1 minute in boiling water. Drain. Place the noodles in a bowl, cover with boiling water and leave for about 4 minutes to hydrate. Drain. Toss with the knob of butter and remaining coriander. Stir the beans into the curry and serve over the noodles.

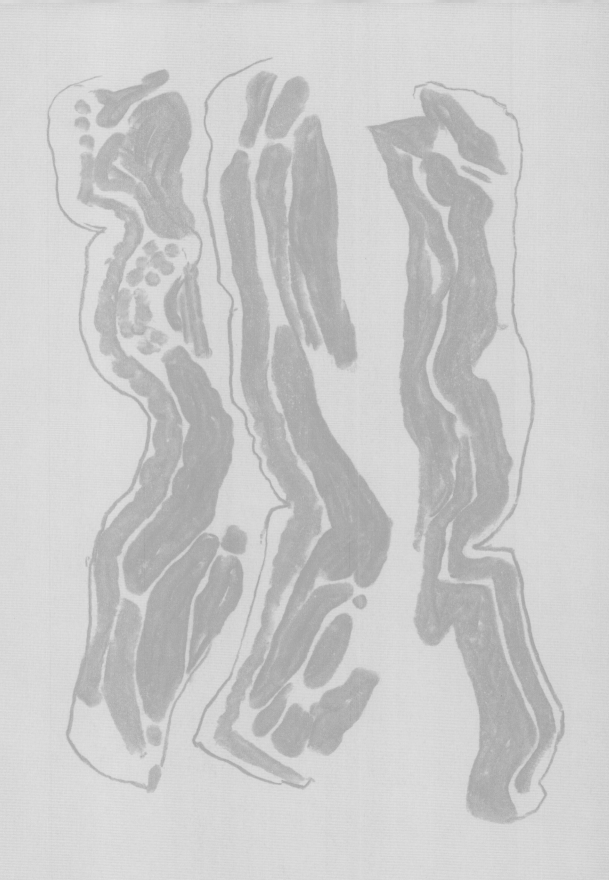

Pork, bacon and ham

Pork can be utterly, utterly delicious, although it is famously difficult to cook well and can be disappointingly dry and tasteless. Some of the best pork dinners I've ever eaten have been at the hand of Chinese cooks because they understand the importance of pork fat. They cook their pork dishes gently and slowly and opt for the fatty cuts from the belly and neck end. Of all meats, the provenance of pork makes the greatest difference to the quality of its flavour and texture. It really pays to buy the best quality you can afford, although given the right cut with appropriate cooking, you can end up with a memorable dinner.

Shoulder meat is fattier than meat from the rear quarters and generally ends up tastier because the fat lubricates the meat as it cooks. It is also cheaper because most people think they want the lean, fast-cooking cuts from the middle (fillet and loin) and rear end (leg fillet and chump chops). Meat from the neck end divides into the hand-and-spring, which is the square of meat at the top of the front leg, and the blade bone, just above it, which gives on to the spare ribs. The hand-and-spring is an old-fashioned cut not stocked by supermarkets but available from butchers. It's very cheap and has great flavour, but needs long, slow cooking; mostly it goes into mince or sausages, both of which need lean and fat. The rib joint is also known as the collar joint and some butchers bone and roll it for roasting or pot-roasting. So-called barbecue ribs (very meaty) and belly slices (like very thick rashers of bacon) are fatty but delicious and suit slow cooking. Surprisingly, they are also good steamed: simply cut the belly into chunks, rub with seasoning and steam in a flat dish for about 10 minutes. The juices will mix with the melted fat to make a sauce. Trotters give stews a wonderful gelatinous texture. Although fatty, pork is a wet meat (like chicken, unlike lamb) and carries a lot of moisture. That's why joints shrink so during cooking. It also means it absorbs marinades easily. Stewing pork is usually diced shoulder – generally blade – boned and diced by the butcher. Fillet can be roasted whole but is best suited to thin slicing and brief frying, finishing perhaps with a dollop of mustard and cream. It is also useful for relatively speedily cooked stewy sorts of dishes.

When it comes to sausages, always choose ones with a high meat content – at least 70 per cent – the sort now called 'butcher's style'. Cured sausage, such as highly seasoned chorizo and pepperoni, is a useful way of using a small amount of meat to inject plenty of flavour into quickly cooked stews, particularly those made with dried beans.

Angostura pork pot

Serves 4   *20 minutes preparation: 35 minutes cooking*

In Trinidad they splash Angostura – the 'pink' in pink gin – into everything and it has an incredible power to 'lift' certain foods. Prawns, for example, tomatoes and chicken, and pineapple and banana are all perked up by a last-minute splash of Angostura bitters. I liked its effect so much that I wrote several recipes using it for my Evening Standard *column, which inspired Angostura to ask me to write a recipe leaflet. This is one of them, a deliciously different, quick-and-easy mid-week supper for friends. Follow with vanilla ice cream splashed with Angostura. Or grill pineapple slices which you've dribbled with Angostura and sprinkled with brown sugar.*

1 large onion
3 garlic cloves
3 tbsp olive oil
400g/14oz pork
100g/3½oz sliced pepperoni
20 small new potatoes
400g/14oz can chickpeas

200g/7oz trimmed green beans
400g/14oz can chopped tomatoes
2 tbsp Angostura bitters
Tabasco sauce (optional)
2 tbsp coarsely chopped coriander
salt and freshly ground pepper

Peel and halve the onion. Finely slice one half and finely chop the other half. Peel the garlic and slice into wafer-thin rounds. Brown the onion in the oil in a large frying pan or similarly wide-based, heavy saucepan placed over a medium heat. Allow about 15 minutes for this, adjusting the heat so the onion doesn't burn. Stir in the garlic and cook for a further 5 minutes.

While the onion and garlic are cooking, cut the pork into kebab-sized chunks and cut the pepperoni in half. Meanwhile, cook the potatoes in salted boiling water. Tip the chickpeas into a sieve under cold running water and shake dry. Cut the beans in half. By now, the onion will be flopped and lightly browned. Push the onion to the side and brown the meat. Add the pepperoni. Cook for a couple of minutes, stirring so all the pepperoni comes into contact with the heat, then add the tomatoes and Angostura. Season with salt and pepper and stir thoroughly. Simmer for about 10 minutes until the pork is cooked through and the tomatoes have thickened and become sauce-like.

Cook the beans in salted boiling water for 2 minutes. Drain. Add the drained potatoes and chickpeas to the stew and simmer until very hot. Taste and adjust the seasoning with salt and pepper. The pepperoni will give the tomato sauce a hit of chilli, but if you want to make the dish hotter, add a few drops of Tabasco. Stir the coriander into the stew. Serve with the beans.

Belly pork with sage, beans and potatoes

Serves 4   *30 minutes preparation: 80 minutes cooking*

Belly pork looks like a thick rasher of streaky bacon. Inevitably it's very fatty, but the good news is that it's cheap and extremely tasty. Its French name – poitrine – sounds far more attractive and over there it's highly regarded for pâtés and terrines, for adding to stews, and making into rillettes. Four of these Desperate Dan rashers make a substantial stew, and in this one the meat is marinated in lemon juice, then cooked with crisply fried garlic. The garlic has a double role in that it flavours the oil in which all the other ingredients are cooked and the crisp flakes make an unusual garnish. Their slightly burnt flavour and crisp texture provide a good contrast to the soft and mild textures and flavours of everything else. All you need with this hearty bowlful is some good crusty bread. Oh, and a brisk walk round the block afterwards.

1 large unwaxed lemon
4 pieces belly pork or flank, about 1kg/2lb
2 large onions
3 garlic cloves
1 tbsp cooking oil
10 sage leaves, finely chopped
400g/14oz can borlotti or other white beans

300ml/½ pint chicken stock, or 150ml/¼ pint white
   wine and 150ml/¼ pint water
450g/14¼oz Charlotte or other small, waxy potatoes
1 tbsp coriander leaves
lemon wedges to serve
salt and freshly ground black pepper

Remove a wafer-thin strip of lemon zest with a potato peeler. Place the pieces of meat on a plate and squeeze over juice from half the lemon. Peel, halve and slice the onions. Peel the garlic and slice in very thin rounds. Heat the oil in a frying pan over a medium heat and when hot, quickly stir-fry the garlic for a few seconds, letting it colour and crisp. Remove from the pan and drain on kitchen paper. Add the meat to the pan and brown for a couple of minutes on both sides. Return to the plate.

Now add the sliced onions to the pan, lower the heat and let them soften, adding the finely chopped sage and, after about 5 minutes, the lemon zest. Tip the beans into a colander and rinse under cold running water. Transfer the onions, sage and lemon zest to a heavy-based, lidded casserole pan. Bury the meat in the onions and pour over any juices and the rinsed beans. Season thoroughly with salt and pepper and add the chosen liquid. Establish a simmer, cover the pan and cook gently for 40 minutes.

Peel the potatoes and, when the cooking time is up, pile them into the pan. Squeeze over the juice from the remaining lemon half, season again and cook on for a further 30 minutes. Remove the lid, raise the heat and boil hard for 10 minutes. Stir in the coriander, sprinkle over the garlic and serve with lemon wedges.

Louisiana red beans and rice

Serves 2–3   *20 minutes preparation: 30 minutes cooking*

It always surprises me how much flavour a small amount of smoked bacon or smoked sausage can give to a dish. Polish kabanos are the secret ingredient of this unpromising-sounding Louisiana-style bean stew. Down South, they are very keen on combining onion with celery, usually with green peppers too, to give their dishes a fresh vivacity. Here the flavours are pepped up with chilli and thyme and the hauntingly delicious beans are served over a mound of previously cooked rice and prettied up with chopped parsley. I like to serve it with my catering-size bottle of Tabasco and chilled beer.

200g/7oz basmati rice
1 onion
3 large garlic cloves
1 red chilli (optional)
1 large celery stick
150g/5oz smoked sausage such as Polish kabanos,
   or ham cut into chunks
1 tbsp cooking oil

1 bay leaf
2 tbsp chopped flat leaf parsley
1 tbsp chopped thyme
400g/14oz can red kidney beans
½ chicken stock cube dissolved in 300ml/½ pint
   boiling water
salt and freshly ground black pepper

Wash the rice, place in a saucepan with a well-fitting lid and cover with 350ml/12fl oz water. Allow to boil, then immediately turn down the heat and clamp on the lid. Cook for 10 minutes, turn off the heat and leave for 10 minutes for the rice to finish cooking in the steam.

While the rice cooks, prepare everything else. Peel and chop the onion and garlic. Split the chilli, if using, scrape away the seeds and chop into tiny dice. Peel the celery and slice across the stick into very thin half moons. Chunk the sausage. Tip the rice into a bowl and keep warm. Wipe out the pan and add the oil. Place over a medium heat and when the oil is hot, stir in the onion, garlic and chilli, if using, with the sausage, celery and bay leaf. Cook briskly, stirring often, until the onion is soft and golden and the sausage has released some of its fat. Chop the parsley. Add the thyme and most of the parsley to the pan and season generously with salt and pepper.

Tip the kidney beans into a sieve and rinse with water. Shake dry and add to the pan. Now add the stock and adjust the heat so the stew simmers steadily for about 10 minutes or until the liquid is reduced and looks more like a sauce. Taste and adjust the seasoning. Stir in the last of the parsley and serve over the rice.

Boston bean soup with watercress

Serves 4 *25 minutes preparation: 35 minutes cooking*

This is one of those useful recipes that relies on a couple of cans from the storecupboard and a few inexpensive easy-to-come-by ingredients. You end up with a thick and robustly flavoured, satisfying soup; the sort of thing that people used to call a rib-sticker. It is even more special when served with a handful of freshly chopped tender green herbs and a generous grating of Parmesan stirred in right at the end. Watercress, or a mixture of flat leaf parsley, mint and chives, gives the soup a noticeable injection of fresh flavour and vivacious colour as well as a healthy dose of iron and vitamins.

2 tbsp olive oil, plus extra to serve
140g/5oz cubed pancetta or chopped streaky bacon
1 large red onion
2 plump garlic cloves
3 carrots
2 celery sticks, with leaves if possible
½ tbsp flour
1 tbsp smooth Dijon mustard
400g/14oz can chopped tomatoes

1 chicken stock cube dissolved in 400ml/14fl oz
    boiling water
squeeze lemon juice
½ tsp Tabasco sauce
400g/14oz can cannellini or haricot beans
75g/3oz watercress
4 tbsp grated Parmesan cheese
salt and freshly ground black pepper

Heat the oil in a spacious, heavy-based saucepan over a medium-low heat. Add the pancetta or streaky bacon and cook until beginning to crisp. Meanwhile, peel, halve and finely chop the onion, garlic and carrots, keeping them in separate piles. When the pancetta is ready, stir in the onion and cook for about 6 minutes until floppy. Add the garlic and carrots. Season lightly with salt and generously with pepper. Cover and cook for 5 minutes, stirring occasionally, adjusting the heat so the vegetables sweat rather than brown.

Trim and finely slice the celery and its leaves and add to the pan. Cook for a minute or two, remove the lid and sift the flour over the top. Stir until it disappears. Now stir in the mustard and add the tomatoes, a little of the stock, a squeeze of lemon juice and Tabasco. Bring to the boil, gradually adding the rest of the stock. Tip the beans into a colander, rinse with cold water, shake dry and add to the pan. Return to a simmer and cook for 10 minutes, or until the vegetables are tender.

Taste and adjust the seasoning. Finely chop the watercress. Just before serving, stir in the watercress and serve each portion with a spoonful of Parmesan and a splosh of best olive oil.

Cocktail sausage and lentil stew

Serves 4   *15 minutes preparation: 45 minutes cooking*

The useful thing about cocktail sausages is that they cook extremely quickly but deliver all the attributes of a first-class banger. Another attractive thing about them is that you get an awful lot of sausage for your money – somehow, half a kilo (1 lb) of cocktail sausages seems so much more than the equivalent of chipolatas or normal-size sausages. They work perfectly in this comforting after-work supper inspired by the Heinz baked beans with sausages that we would occasionally get as children as a teatime treat. The lentil version is great with a chunk of bread and a green bean salad made by dicing a shallot and stirring it into a mayonnaise-based vinaigrette dressing and pouring it over halved and briefly boiled stick beans.

1 large red onion
2 large garlic cloves
2 tbsp olive oil
500g/1lb good-quality cocktail sausages
1 large flat brown mushroom

150g/5oz Puy lentils
400g/14oz can peeled plum tomatoes
½ stock cube dissolved in 300ml/½ pint hot water
squeeze lemon juice
salt and freshly ground black pepper

Peel the onion and garlic. Cut the onion lengthways into quarters and slice thinly across each quarter; finely slice the garlic. Heat the oil in a medium-sized saucepan that can hold all the ingredients placed over a medium heat. Stir in the onion. Cook, stirring often, for about 5 minutes until beginning to wilt.

Meanwhile, cut the links between the sausages if necessary. Add the garlic to the pan and, a couple of minutes later, increase the heat and stir in the sausages. Cook, stirring every so often, for 10 minutes until the sausages are browned on all sides.

Wipe the mushroom and cut into small dice. Stir the mushroom and then the lentils into the pan. Cook for a couple of minutes and then add the tomatoes to the stew. Bring the juices to the boil while breaking up the tomatoes with a wooden spoon. Add the stock, return to the boil, then reduce the heat, partially cover the pan and simmer gently for about 30 minutes.

Season the dish when the lentils are tender. Adjust the flavours with a squeeze of lemon juice. This stew reheats perfectly and, as is so often the case with lentil-based dishes, I think it tastes even better the next day.

Dublin coddle

Serves 4   *15 minutes preparation: 30 minutes cooking*

Coddle is another word for cuddle and this is what you get from this comforting Irish sausage stew: the culinary equivalent of a cuddle. It's the ideal lazy cook's supper because you do nothing except put everything in a pot and let it bubble or coddle away with minimal attention. The smells that waft round the kitchen are unbelievably good and the results really do live up to expectations. Any meaty pork sausages are perfect for this dish, but I chose slim sausages to speed up what is usually a long, slow dish, left for hours on the back burner. If using regular sausages, increase the stewing time to 45 minutes.

4 onions, about 450g/14½oz
8 good-sized potatoes, about 750g/1½lb
8 rashers rindless streaky bacon
625g/1¼lb slim pork sausages/chipolatas

250g/8oz frozen peas or spring greens
handful flat leaf parsley leaves
50g/2oz cold butter (optional)
salt and freshly ground black pepper

Peel, halve and finely chop the onions. Peel the potatoes, chop into bite-sized chunks, rinse and shake dry. Place the onions and potatoes in a 2-litre/3½-pint-capacity, heavy-based, lidded saucepan. Cut the bacon rashers into pieces and add them too.

Season generously with salt and black pepper, add 600ml/1 pint cold water and lay the sausages on top, pushing them under as best you can. Place the pan over a high heat and bring to the boil. Reduce the heat immediately, establish a steady but gentle simmer, cover the pan and cook for 20 minutes. Remove the lid, increase the heat and boil for 10 minutes.

Meanwhile, finely shred the spring greens, if using, place in a colander and rinse thoroughly with cold water. Shake dry. Coarsely chop the parsley. Add the frozen peas or spring greens to the pan, poking them down under the liquid. Cook for 5 minutes. Stir the parsley into the pan. Taste the liquid and add salt if necessary. Serve in wide soup bowls, adding a knob of cold butter, if liked, to thicken and enrich the sauce.

Huevos a la flamenca

Serves 2   *20 minutes preparation: 30 minutes cooking*

Tomatoes with eggs is one of my favourite combinations of food, and one which I like in many forms. This gutsy, robust tomato and egg dish is a speciality of Seville and it's something that everyone cooks slightly differently. I like it with chorizo and Spanish cured ham, as well as roasted piquillo peppers, and I've taken recently to cooking it with smoked as opposed to ordinary paprika. Peas give this combo a sweet freshness that works extremely well and the dish is uplifted with plenty of flat-leaf parsley. The eggs are added right at the end and are poached in the stew until the white is set. Traditionally this is done in the oven, but I find it simpler to do over direct heat with a lid on the pan. Serve with plenty of crusty bread and butter. A cold beer or a bottle of a decent Rioja would be perfect accompaniments. Roasted piquillo peppers, stocked by most supermarkets, aren't essential to the success of the dish but enrich it greatly.

100g/3½oz sliced chorizo
4 slices Serrano or Parma ham
1 red onion
1 plump garlic clove
splash olive oil
500g/1lb fresh tomatoes or 400g/14oz can
    chopped tomatoes

3 roasted pimiento piquillo red peppers
1 tsp sweet smoked paprika or regular 'noble sweet'
    paprika
100g/3½oz frozen petits pois (optional)
handful flat leaf parsley
4 eggs
salt and freshly ground black pepper

Choose a spacious frying pan and gently fry the chorizo without any oil – it will produce plenty – until crusty on both sides. Make a pile of the ham, fold it in half and slice thickly. Stir the ham into the chorizo. Remove the chorizo and ham to a plate, tipping the pan so as much oil as possible remains in the pan.

Meanwhile, peel, halve and finely chop the onion and garlic. Add a splash of olive oil to the pan and cook the onion and garlic for about 10 minutes until obviously beginning to soften. If using fresh tomatoes, pour boiling water over them. Count to 20, drain, peel and coarsely chop. Split the peppers, scrape away the seeds and slice chunkily. Add the tomatoes, paprika, a generous seasoning of salt and pepper and the piquillo peppers to the pan and cook briskly for about 10 minutes until united into a thick sauce.

Return the chorizo and ham. Now add the peas, if using, and cook for 3–4 minutes until just tender. Roughly chop the parsley and stir most of it into the stew. Make 4 indentations and crack the eggs directly into them. Cover the pan and cook for about 5 minutes until the egg whites are just set. Serve immediately with the remaining parsley over the top.

Jambalaya

Serves 3–4 *20 minutes preparation: 50 minutes cooking*

Jambalaya is a rice, meat and seafood stew from Louisiana. Traditionally the cooking starts with the so-called 'trinity' of onion, green pepper and celery which begins many dishes from the Deep South, but thereafter almost anything goes. The name is a jumble of jambon, *the French word for ham, and* alaya, *which means rice in an African dialect, and consequently the dish usually includes a spicy pork sausage of some sort, although often ends up with ham. Whatever the ingredients, a good jambalaya is always spiked with plenty of chilli. My version of this easygoing dish is made even more colourful with red onions and red peppers and I have purposely restrained the chilli-heat by using cayenne at the beginning of the cooking and adding Tabasco towards the end, while serving Tabasco and a wedge of lemon alongside so that people can adjust the dish to suit their own heat threshold. A good supply of ice-cold beer is essential.*

2 red onions, about 275g/9oz
2 plump garlic cloves
1 red pepper
1 celery heart
2 tbsp cooking oil
1 bay leaf
½ tsp cayenne pepper
2 large skinless boned chicken thighs
2 pepperoni sausages or 50g/2oz sliced chorizo

200g/7oz raw giant tiger prawns with shells
½ tsp Tabasco sauce
250g/8oz basmati rice
400g/14oz can whole Italian tomatoes
1 chicken stock cube dissolved in 500ml/17fl oz
   water
1 tbsp finely chopped parsley
1 lemon (for wedges)
salt and freshly ground black pepper

Peel and chop the onions and garlic. Core, deseed and dice the red pepper. Trim and slice the celery, setting aside the leaves, rinse and drain. Heat the oil in a 2-litre/3½-pint heavy-based flameproof casserole and stir in the onion and garlic. Cook for about 5 minutes then add the red pepper, celery and bay leaf. Season with salt and pepper and cayenne and cook for about 10 minutes more while you prepare everything else.

Cut the chicken into chunks. Slice the pepperoni chunkily or halve the chorizo. If the prawns are frozen, slip into warm water for about 5 minutes and remove the shells. Place the prawns in a bowl and toss with the Tabasco. Stir the chicken into the vegetables and, when it's changed colour, add the pepperoni, if using, the rice and the canned tomatoes with their juice. Add the stock. Bring to a simmer, cover the pan and cook for 20 minutes.

By now the rice will have absorbed most of the liquid but the jambalaya should be nicely moist. If it isn't, add a little more stock. Stir in the prawns, cover the pan again and cook for 10 more minutes. Sprinkle over the celery leaves and parsley and serve with lemon wedges and the Tabasco bottle.

Chorizo and white bean stew

Serves 2   *15 minutes preparation: 15 minutes cooking*

In Barcelona's famous La Boqueria market there is a fabulous little stall devoted to beans. White beans, black beans, kidney-shaped beans and oval beans – it's hard to choose which ones to use for the inevitable chorizo or butifarra *stew. I don't know anywhere in the UK that sells cooked beans as they do, so I turned to a can of cannellini beans for this approximation of a spicy Iberian bean stew. It's the sort of dish which can be expanded to fuel larger appetites or an extra mouth, by adding a few chunks of boiled potato. Serve hot from the pan with crusty bread and a chilled beer or lukewarm over shredded Little Gem lettuce hearts with a slice of garlic-rubbed toast dribbled with olive oil. Chilled dry fino or a glass of white wine would be my choice with the latter.*

2 rashers rindless streaky bacon
1 onion
2 plump garlic cloves
2 tbsp olive oil
1 bay leaf
2 tomatoes
400g/14oz can cannellini beans

1 tsp chopped rosemary
½ tsp chopped thyme
1 tsp paprika
3 x 10cm/4in cooked chorizo
2 tbsp chopped flat leaf parsley
salt and freshly ground black pepper

Slice the bacon across the rashers into strips. Peel and chop the onion. Peel and finely chop the garlic. Heat 1 tablespoon of the olive oil in a heavy-based medium-sized saucepan placed over a medium heat. Add the bacon and bay leaf and cook for a couple of minutes until the fat begins to run. Add the onion and cook, stirring frequently, for 3–4 minutes adjusting the heat slightly so it browns without burning.

Chop the tomatoes. Tip the beans into a sieve and rinse thoroughly with cold water. Shake dry. Add the garlic, rosemary and thyme to the pan and cook until aromatic. Stir in the paprika, then add the tomatoes. Cook, reducing the heat slightly, until the tomatoes have flopped to give a small amount of juice.

While that's happening, slice the chorizo intp approximately 1cm/½in-wide pieces. Add to the pan. Add the beans together with a generous seasoning of salt and pepper. Pour in 100ml/3½fl oz water and simmer for 5 minutes. Taste and adjust the seasoning. Stir in the parsley and the remaining olive oil. This stew will keep covered in the fridge for several days.

Oeufs landaise

Serves 2   *15 minutes preparation: 35 minutes cooking*

It was my eminent predecessor as Evening Standard *cookery writer, X. Marcel Boulestin's idea to call sausage hash* oeufs landaise. *He is one of my culinary heroes, with his conviction that good food should be a natural part of our daily life. He hated waste, believed in using up leftovers, and eating seasonally. He also understood the importance of simplicity. This is my version of Boulestin's sausage hash.*

1 large onion
2 tbsp vegetable oil
6 good-quality pork sausages
3 tomatoes
8 small potatoes, boiled
1 small apple

4 sage leaves or pinch dried sage
2 eggs
handful grated Cheddar cheese
1 tbsp chopped parsley
salt and freshly ground black pepper

Peel, halve and finely chop the onion. Fry the onion in the oil in a frying pan, cooking briskly and stirring often, until browned in places and beginning to soften – about 10 minutes.

Meanwhile, slash the sausages and remove the skin. Break them into small pieces. Place the tomatoes in a bowl and cover with boiling water. Count to 20, drain, cut out the core in a small cone shape and quarter lengthways. Scrape out the seeds and chop the tomato flesh. Chop the potatoes into chunky dice. Peel, quarter, core and chop the apple. Finely shred the sage, if using fresh leaves.

Add the pieces of sausage to the partially cooked onion, adjusting the heat and stirring occasionally so the sausage browns and cooks through. After about 10 minutes stir in the sage and add the potatoes and apple. Cook for a further 10 minutes until everything is browned, season with salt and pepper and add the tomatoes. Cook for 1 more minute.

Break the eggs into the hash, cover the pan and return the pan to the heat until the egg white firms. Sprinkle the cheese over the top. For a gratin finish, pop the hash under a pre-heated grill; it is ready when the cheese begins to bubble but before the egg yolk hardens. Sprinkle with the chopped parsley and serve from the pan.

Polish pork with pickled cabbage and dill

Serves 4   *20 minutes preparation: 45 minutes cooking*

Friday night, when for many the working week is over, is switch-off time. Sometimes it's just the ticket to slob around at home, cooking something easy to share with friends. Stewy dishes, the sort that simmer away on the back burner filling the house with good smells while you pour yourself a drink or two, always go down well. Often they are off-putting to make because they can take an age to cook. Not this one. It is also easy to shop for, mindless to prepare and it reheats perfectly. This hauntingly flavoured dish also manages to be both comforting and a bit special. Slices of crispy fried smoked pork sausage stirred into the thick, luscious, terracotta-coloured sauce and a final garnish of soured cream with spikes of bright green dill, make this a supper you won't forget in a hurry. Serve alone with bread or make it go further with mashed potato. You will definitely need a bottle of full-bodied red wine.

75g/3oz diced pancetta or smoked bacon pieces
2 tbsp lard or vegetable oil
1 large onion
2 garlic cloves
2 pork shoulder steaks, about 500g/1lb
1 tsp caraway seeds
1 heaped tbsp sweet paprika

1 chicken stock cube dissolved in 500ml/17fl oz
    boiling water
500g/1lb jar sauerkraut
2 tbsp coarsely chopped dill
275g/9oz carton soured cream
250g/8oz smoked pork sausage
salt

Choose a medium-sized, heavy-based pan and fry the bacon in 1 tablespoon of the lard or oil for about 5 minutes until crisp. Peel and dice the onion and garlic and add them to the pan. Cook, stirring occasionally, for 6–7 minutes, or until tender. Cut the pork into kebab-sized chunks. Stir the caraway and diced meat into the pan and brown the meat all over. Add the paprika, cooking it for 30 seconds, and then add the hot stock. Bring to the boil, reduce the heat immediately, cover the pan and simmer for 10 minutes.

Drain the sauerkraut and add it and 1½ tablespoons of the dill to the pan. Return the liquid to the boil, while stirring thoroughly, then reduce the heat, cover the pan and cook for about 20 minutes or until the meat and sauerkraut are tender. Stir ½ teaspoon salt and half the soured cream into the pan. Ten minutes before you're ready to eat, slice the pork sausage thickly and fry it briskly in the remaining lard or oil until nicely crusty. Stir the sausage into the stew, check the seasoning and serve with a dollop of soured cream, garnished with the remaining dill.

Pork tenderloin with beer

Serves 4   *30 minutes preparation: 45–60 minutes cooking*

Pork can be annoyingly difficult to cook well. Too often it ends up dry, dull, surprisingly tough and unimpressed by interesting flavour enhancers. One cut that's hard to spoil is pork fillet. Here, little scraps of lemon zest and occasional bursts of sage, with a background creaminess and heat from Dijon mustard, enliven what is essentially a gentle, comforting sort of dish. It doesn't really need an accompaniment, but you could add small, boiled new potatoes for the last 5 minutes of cooking, otherwise mash is always good with a dish like this.

1 large onion
2 large garlic cloves
8 large sage leaves
1 small unwaxed lemon
3 tbsp olive oil

400g/14oz pork fillet
1 tbsp smooth Dijon mustard
250ml/8fl oz light beer
400g/14oz can butter or cannellini beans
salt and freshly ground black pepper

Peel, halve and finely slice the onion. Peel the garlic and slice in wafer-thin rounds. Place the sage leaves on top of each other and shred as thinly as possible. Remove the zest from the lemon in postage-stamp-size scraps without a hint of white pith. Heat the olive oil in a large frying pan or a similarly wide-based saucepan and add the onion, garlic, sage and lemon zest. Cook gently, stirring often, for at least 10 minutes, probably 15–20, or until the onion is floppy, golden and scorched in places.

Meanwhile, cut the pork into large kebab-sized pieces. Add the meat to the pan and increase the heat. Turn the pieces of meat regularly until browned all over. Season with salt and pepper and stir in the mustard. Add the beer, stirring as it comes to the boil, then reduce the heat so the liquid simmers very gently. Cover the pan and cook for 20 minutes.

Tip the beans into a sieve, rinse with cold water, shake dry and add to the pan. Cook uncovered for 10 minutes or so to reduce and thicken the gravy. Taste and adjust the seasoning with salt and pepper if necessary before serving.

Portuguese pork

Serves 2 *15 minutes preparation: 20 minutes cooking*

The Portuguese are big on salt cod, chilli, beans and chickpeas. I've called this dish Portuguese pork because it is made with some of these ingredients and a few others that are popular in Portuguese cooking, such as garlic, onion, pork and fresh coriander. It is a quickly made, fresh-tasting and, above all, interesting stew which makes good use of pork fillet. I like to serve this with small new potatoes, cooked and then added to the pot at the end of cooking, but it is great as it is with a chunk of crusty bread. There again, rice would be good.

200g/7oz pork fillet
½ tsp ground cumin
juice of 1 small lemon
1 large red onion
3 tbsp olive oil
3 plump garlic cloves

1 small red chilli
400g/14oz can chickpeas
½ chicken stock cube dissolved in 250ml/8fl oz
    boiling water
large bunch coriander at least 75g/3oz
salt and freshly ground black pepper

Chop the pork into pieces slightly smaller than you would if you were making kebabs. Place in a bowl and sprinkle over the cumin. Squeeze over the lemon juice and toss. Peel, halve and finely chop the onion. Heat the olive oil in a pan large enough to accommodate the entire dish over a medium heat. Add the onion and cook, stirring every now and again, so that it softens and colours slightly. Cook for 10 minutes.

Meanwhile, peel the garlic and chop quite small. Split the chilli, scrape away the seeds and membrane and chop very small. Add the garlic and chilli to the onion. Cook for a further 5 minutes, stirring every now and again. Tip the chickpeas into a sieve, rinse thoroughly with cold water and shake dry. Scoop the pork out of its lemon bath, raise the heat slightly, and stir it into the onion.

Stir constantly as the pork changes colour. Add the chickpeas, stock and cumin-flavoured lemon juice left behind in the bowl. Bring everything to the boil, simmer gently, stir well, taste and season thoroughly (it will need it) with salt and pepper. Pick the coriander leaves from the stalks, chop roughly and stir into the stew. Simmer for a moment or two and serve.

Pork noodles with wilted spinach

Serves 4   *15 minutes preparation: 10 minutes cooking*

This simple, slurpy noodle supper is a good example of how easy it is to make quite ordinary, everyday ingredients into a healthy, delicious and satisfying dish. The classic oriental trinity of garlic, chilli and ginger injects serious flavour, while rice wine and fresh coriander combine with soy sauce to turn this quick and easy dish into a cross between a Vietnamese-style noodle soup-supper and a Thai stir-fry.

600ml/1 pint chicken stock
200g/7oz dried rice sticks (tagliatelle-style)
1 bunch spring onions, about 125g/4oz
1 plump garlic clove
1 small red chilli
5cm/2in piece fresh ginger
200g/7oz pork escalope

100g/3½oz young spinach leaves
1½ tbsp sesame oil
2 tbsp sherry or rice wine
handful coarsely chopped coriander leaves
soy sauce to serve
salt and freshly ground black pepper

Bring the chicken stock to the boil in a medium-sized saucepan. Taste and season with salt and pepper. Soak the noodles, covered, for 4 minutes in boiling water. Drain then add them to the simmering stock and cook for a couple of minutes. Turn off the heat and cover the pan.

Trim and slice the spring onions, including all but the damaged or very tough green ends. Peel the garlic and chop finely. Split the chilli, scrape out the seeds, slice into thin batons and chop into tiny dice. Peel the ginger and grate or slice into very thin small batons. Slice across the grain of the escalopes, cutting the meat into 3cm/1½in-long strips.

Bunch the spinach up in your hand and slice through it a few times to shred coarsely. Heat a wok or large frying pan over a high heat. Add the oil and swirl it round the pan. Lift the wok off the heat, add the prepared spring onions, garlic, chilli and ginger, and stir-fry for a few seconds before returning to the heat. Continue cooking for about 1 minute, reducing the heat so nothing burns, then add the strips of meat. Toss around for a couple of minutes, again adjusting the heat so the food cooks quickly but without burning. Add the sherry or rice wine and allow almost to boil away until sticky. Stir the shredded spinach into the pan, tossing everything around for a few moments as the spinach wilts. Remove the pan from the heat.

Scoop the noodles into deep bowls and sprinkle with all but 1 tablespoon of the coriander but reserve about 1 tablespoonful. Pour on the stock and top with the meat and spinach mixture. Garnish with the remaining coriander and serve with soy sauce, forks and spoons.

Sausage and mushroom cassoulet

Serves 4   *15 minutes preparation: 25 minutes cooking*

This is nothing like a real cassoulet. There is no preserved goose in this version; in fact the only common ingredients are sausages (which have a minor role in the Real Thing) and haricot beans. However, the dish looks somewhat similar and is grounded in the same sort of idea whereby sausages and other ingredients are stewed together in a rich and robustly flavoured wine gravy. This 'cassoulet' is stunningly easy to make and is just the sort of stew-up that wards off the chilly blast of winter. If you are really big eaters, add some chunks of boiled potato and a handful of frozen peas. Serve in deep bowls and pass the mustard.

500g/1lb good-quality pork sausages
1 tbsp cooking oil (optional)
1 large red onion
2 plump garlic cloves
8 medium closed cap mushrooms
3 tbsp olive oil
1 bay leaf

1 tsp thyme leaves
2 glasses red wine, about 300ml/½ pint
squirt tomato ketchup
400g/14oz can haricot beans
400g/14oz can green lentils
squeeze lemon
salt and freshly ground black pepper

Begin by setting the sausages to cook in your favourite way. Don't prick them and if frying (in 1 tablespoon cooking oil) or grilling, cook over a moderate heat turning frequently as they begin to turn crusty and brown. Reckon on about 15 minutes' cooking.

Meanwhile, peel and halve the onion. Slice down the halves to make chunky half moons. Crack the garlic cloves with your fist, flake away the skins and chop. Wipe the mushrooms and cut into quarters. Heat the olive oil in a frying pan over a medium heat and cook the onion, adding the garlic after 5 minutes. Add the mushrooms, bay leaf and thyme leaves, season generously with salt and pepper and continue to cook for a further 5 minutes. Add the wine and ketchup, let it bubble up, then reduce the heat to a simmer.

Tip the haricots and lentils into a sieve, rinse under cold running water, shake dry and add to the pan. Season again and cook for 5 more minutes or until the mushrooms are done to your liking. By now the sausages should be ready. Add them whole to the stew or cut into small chipolata-sized pieces. Taste and adjust the seasoning with salt, pepper and a squeeze of lemon.

Spezzatino

Serves 4   *20 minutes preparation: 30 minutes cooking*

Pork fillet isn't the most economical cut but it does always give good results. Take this Spanish-style stew. It's hard to believe that such a robust, full-bodied dish takes as little as 30 minutes to cook. It's one of those wonderful meal-in-a-bowl dishes that's full of lively, fresh flavours and the meat ends up tender and juicy. I like to serve it with plenty of crusty bread.

500g/1lb small new potatoes such as Charlotte
about 400g/14oz pork fillet
1 large red onion
1 red chilli
1 large garlic clove
1 unwaxed lemon

3 tbsp olive oil
300ml/½ pint white wine or water
400g/14oz can chickpeas
generous handful coriander leaves
150g/5oz young spinach
salt and freshly ground black pepper

Scrub or peel the potatoes and boil in plenty of salted water. Meanwhile, trim any fatty sinew from the pork and cut into kebab-sized chunks. Peel and halve the onion and slice down the halves to make chunky half moons. Trim and split the chilli, wipe away the seeds and slice into small scraps. Peel the garlic and finely chop or slice into wafer-thin rounds. Use a potato peeler to remove the zest from the lemon in paper-thin 3cm/1½in lengths.

Heat the olive oil in a spacious frying pan or similarly wide-based saucepan and stir in the onion. Adjust the heat so it flops and softens, and browns in places without burning. After about 10 minutes add the chilli, garlic and lemon zest and cook on, stirring often, for a further 2–3 minutes until the garlic is aromatic and beginning to change colour. Increase the heat slightly and cook the meat in batches, letting it brown all over before cooking the next batch. Adding it thus, instead of all at once, avoids the meat sweating instead of browning.

Return the browned meat to the pan, then add the wine or water and cook at a steady simmer for 10–15 minutes until the meat is cooked through. Tip the chickpeas into a sieve, rinse under cold running water, shake dry and add to the pan. Heat through, taste and adjust the seasoning with salt, pepper and lemon juice. Coarsely chop the coriander and stir it into the stew together with the spinach. By now the potatoes will be cooked. Drain them and add to the pan. Stir and serve very hot as soon as the spinach has wilted.

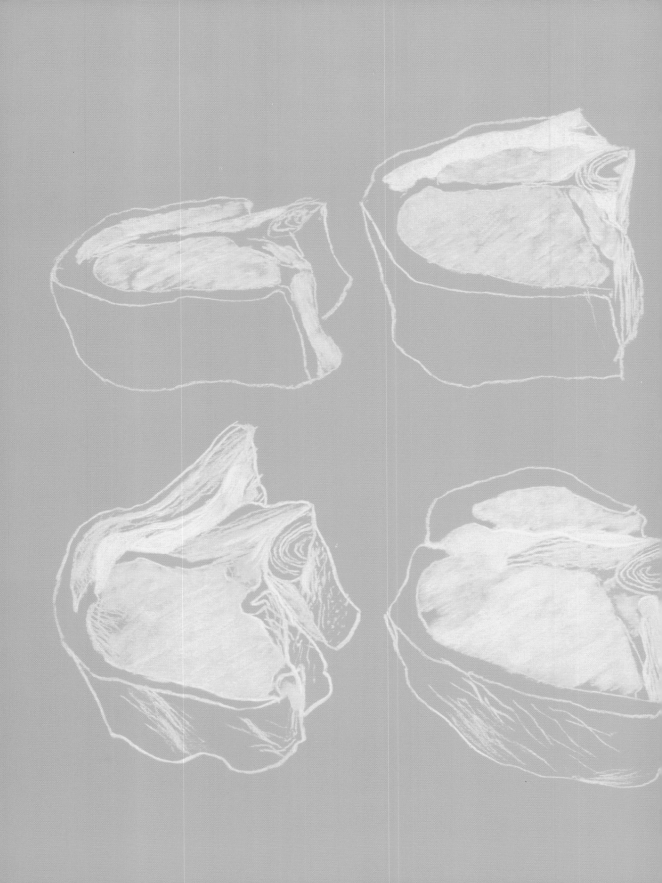

Lamb

It's hard to cook lamb badly. According to my butcher, the most popular cut is lamb fillet. It is ideal for quickly cooked dishes and perfect for kebabs because the fat running through it lubricates and flavours the meat. It is also a good but expensive choice for stewed dishes. Shoulder or middle neck chops are perfect for braising, and boned and diced, fat-trimmed shoulder meat is good for stews and casseroles. Scrag or neck on the bone has great flavour and is one of the least expensive cuts, but you do sometimes get splintery bones. A proportion of bone gives the meat plenty of flavour. The bony cuts are always the cheapest. Shanks – a cheap, unknown cut until the first *River Café Cook Book* championed them – provide plenty of delicious lean meat but are superb left on the bone and cooked slowly, buried in a mound of finely sliced onion.

You can never go wrong with leg of lamb. Many people think they prefer it because it is far leaner than shoulder. It is usefully versatile and is as good for fast, pan-fried dishes as it is for slowly cooked stews and casseroles. Leg steaks and fillets can be delicious cooked simply and eaten in a meat-and-two-veg kind of a way. In summer it is worth looking out for salt-marsh lamb reared on coastal salt marshes. Its unique salty flavour is highly prized in France and a speciality from Mont St Michel in Normandy where it's known as *prés-salé*.

I tend to buy chump chops, which are fatty but rich in flavour, for stews, although it's sometimes possible to pick up bargains at the supermarket on bumper packs of loin chops and skinny cutlets cut from the best end of neck. Having said that, I rarely buy lamb from the supermarket. I prefer the wider selection of cuts and the freedom to buy the quantity that suits me and not the supermarket, which is offered by my butcher. All his lamb is free-range and properly hung, thus ensuring a robust lamby flavour and properly tender meat. Farmers' Markets are another excellent source of good-quality, often local, lamb.

Cocido of lamb with coriander

Serves 4   *20 minutes preparation: 45 minutes cooking*

Cocido is the collective name for Spanish stews. They are cooked gently for several hours until the meat is tender and infused with flavour in a pot-bellied, earthenware crock with the equally distinctive name of olla. Cocidos always include dried chickpeas and my after-work version speeds up the cooking with canned chickpeas. There's a background hint of heat from paprika and the stew is thickened and coloured with canned tomatoes, then finished with shredded spinach and coriander leaves. Serve it on its own with a chunk of bread. Boiled potatoes would be a good accompaniment too.

2 garlic cloves
3 tbsp olive oil
500g/1lb boneless lamb leg steaks diced
1 red onion
400g/14oz can chopped tomatoes
½ tsp paprika

1 tbsp tomato purée
400g/14oz can chickpeas
150g/5oz young spinach leaves
generous handful coriander leaves
salt and freshly ground black pepper

Peel and coarsely chop the garlic. Sprinkle it with a generous pinch of salt and use the flat of a knife to work to a juicy paste. Mix the paste with 1 tablespoon of the olive oil and smear the mixture all over the meat.

Leave to marinate while you peel and quarter the onion. Slice across the quarters very thinly and fry in the remaining oil in a large frying pan or similarly wide-based saucepan. Cook briskly, stirring often, for about 6 minutes until the onion is juicy, wilted and beginning to brown. Season generously with salt and pepper, turn down the heat and cook for a further 4–5 minutes, then tip the juicy, browning onion onto a plate.

Return the pan to a medium-high heat and quickly brown the meat in batches so that it turns crusty rather than sweats in the pan. Return the onion to the meat and add the can of chopped tomatoes. Give everything a good stir, scraping up all the crusty bits, then tip the stew into a heavy-based medium-sized saucepan. Half fill the empty tomato can with water and add that to the pan together with the paprika and tomato purée. Bring the stew to the boil, half cover the pan and simmer steadily for 20 minutes.

Tip the chickpeas into a sieve, rinse with cold water, shake dry and add to the pan. Taste the juices and season with salt and pepper. Check that the meat is tender; if not, simmer for a further 10 minutes or so. Shred the spinach, coarsely chop the coriander and stir both into the pan. When the spinach has wilted, the dish is ready.

Frito mallorquin

Serves 4   *20 minutes preparation: 45 minutes cooking*

The dish I kept hearing about on my first trip to Majorca was Frito Mallorquin. Properly made, it should include the full complement of lamb bits, the kidney, lungs, heart and sweetbreads as well as the liver, and be thickened with its blood. But don't be alarmed: mine is a gentler version made only with the liver. I suspect it's one of those dishes that varies from cook to cook, but the basis for my recipe is one I sampled at Jaume in Deia, an appetite-raising walk from Sa Padrissa where we were staying. We ate it watching the sun go down on a terrace overlooking the curve of a mountain grounded by spots of light from the road. It's a hearty, robust dish by any standards, and not the sort of thing you expect to be eating after a day in the sun. But its juicy texture and complex flavours make it one of those meal-in-a-bowl dishes that is irresistible whatever the weather.

500g/1lb Jersey Royal or new potatoes
6 tbsp olive oil
3 large garlic cloves
1 red onion
1 bay leaf
400g/14oz lamb's liver
1 aubergine, about 400g/14oz
4 roasted piquillo pimiento red peppers or
  2 roasted red peppers

½ tsp chilli flakes
generous pinch ground allspice or of cinnamon
  and cloves
225g/7½oz shelled broad beans or fresh or
  frozen peas
1 tbsp chopped marjoram
salt and freshly ground black pepper

Scrub or peel the potatoes and boil in salted water in a spacious heavy based flameproof casserole until tender. Drain and cut into even-sized chunks. Heat 3 tablespoons of the oil in a frying pan and cook the potatoes slowly until crusty. Meanwhile, peel and finely slice the garlic. Peel and finely chop the onion. Remove potatoes from the casserole and heat 3 more tablespoons of oil. Stir in the garlic. Cook for a few seconds until aromatic, then stir in the onion. Add the bay leaf and cook, stirring occasionally, until the onion is soft.

Meanwhile, cut the liver into tiny dice; discard any sinew. Trim the aubergine and cut into dice about the size of sugar lumps. Split the peppers, remove the seeds and chop into short strips. Stir the liver into the onions, increase the heat and stir constantly until it loses its pinkness.

Add the aubergine, which will seem a large amount, but softens and shrinks. Reduce the heat. Stir well. Add the chilli flakes, allspice or cinnamon and cloves, and the peppers. Season with lots of salt and pepper. Cover; cook for 20 minutes until the liver and aubergine are very tender.

Cook the beans in salted water for 3 minutes. Drain and, if liked (I do), remove their rubbery sheaths. If using peas, cook until just tender. Stir the beans or peas and potatoes into the pan. Add the marjoram and serve.

Cumin lamb and aubergine stew

Serves 4   *25 minutes preparation: 35 minutes cooking*

If you're craving comfort food with attitude, I thoroughly recommend this Greek-inspired stew. Chunks of tender lamb fillet are hauntingly spiced with the unlikely-sounding combination of balsamic vinegar and cumin and held in a rich tomato sauce, which is thick with meltingly tender pieces of aubergine. This beguilingly flavoured stew is lifted with the last-minute addition of fresh mint and offset by a scoop of creamy Greek yoghurt. In Greece they are very fond of serving stews with a tiny pasta called risi, named after its rice-like shape. Any of the small, so-called soup pastas would be perfect with this stew but, if you prefer, it goes very well with couscous or rice. Although the stew is relatively fast to cook, it is the sort of dish that improves with reheating and will probably taste even better tomorrow.

375g/12oz lamb neck fillet	400g/14oz can chopped tomatoes
2 heaped tsp ground cumin	1 tbsp balsamic vinegar
1 aubergine, about 200g/7oz	15g/½oz bunch fresh mint
1 large red onion	150g/5oz Greek yoghurt
1 large garlic clove	salt and freshly ground black pepper
2 tbsp olive oil	

Cut the lamb into chunks slightly smaller than kebab size. Dust with the cumin. Trim the aubergine and cut into similar-sized pieces. Peel the onion, cut in half and dice finely. Peel and finely chop the garlic. Heat the olive oil in a 2-litre/3½-pint-capacity, heavy-based, lidded saucepan and stir in the onion and garlic. Cook for 5 minutes over a medium heat, stirring regularly.

Add the aubergine and quickly toss all the pieces in the oily onion. Reduce the heat and cook, stirring a couple of times, for 5 minutes until the aubergine begins to soften. Increase the heat and add the lamb, browning it thoroughly. Season with salt and pepper and add the tomatoes and balsamic vinegar. Half fill the empty tomato can with water and add that too. Bring to the boil, reduce the heat immediately, three-quarters cover the pan and establish a steady simmer. Cook for 20 minutes.

Check the meat is tender and continue cooking for a further 5–10 minutes if necessary. Coarsely chop the mint and stir most of it into the stew. Check the seasoning and serve with a dollop of yoghurt and a sprinkling of the last of the mint.

Lamb and noodle stir-fry with ginger

Serves 2 *15 minutes preparation: 15 minutes cooking*

I have an on/off relationship with my wok. It hangs, unloved and gathering dust, for months on end and then for no apparent reason I use it night after night-after-night. Stir-fries, which are what most people use their wok for, never go out of fashion because they are quick, easy and endlessly variable. This one is simply seasoned with the winning combination of garlic and ginger and given a Chinese imprint with sherry and soy sauce. Thai-style rice noodles, which need merely to be rehydrated before they are ready to eat, are perfect for quick stir-fries but any noodles would work well.

175g/6oz rice sticks/rice noodles
250g/8oz boneless lamb leg steaks
150g/5oz mangetout
1 leek
1 large garlic clove
5cm/2in piece fresh ginger

2 large carrots, about 250g/8oz
4 tbsp sesame oil
1 tbsp sherry
1 tbsp soy sauce
handful coriander leaves

Place the rice sticks in a bowl or pan and cover with boiling water. Leave for 5 minutes, rinse and drain. Slice the meat into thin strips about 5 x 0.5cm/2 x ¼in. Slice the mangetout on the diagonal into four pieces. Trim the leek and thinly slice on the diagonal; rinse and shake dry. Peel and finely chop the garlic. Peel the ginger and slice into skinny batons. Peel the carrots and thinly slice on the diagonal.

Heat 3 tablespoons of the oil in a wok or large frying pan over the highest heat and swirl it round the pan. Add the leek, tossing it as it begins to wilt. Add the ginger and garlic and then the carrots. Stir-fry for a couple of minutes, then add the sherry and mangetout.

Keep the food moving for a couple of minutes, then scrape it to the side to make way for the meat. Add the remaining oil and the lamb. Cook without moving for a couple of minutes until crusty. Turn, cook for another 30 seconds or so, then sprinkle with soy sauce and mix with the vegetables. Add the coriander, give one final toss and turn off the heat. Drain the rice sticks, pile into bowls and top with a share of the stir fry. Serve with soy sauce and, if you have some, a dribble of toasted sesame oil.

Irish stew

Serves 6   *20 minutes preparation: 90 minutes cooking*

I'm not Irish, but with an Irish builder in what seems like permanent residence, I'm beginning to feel it. He's a bit special is Dermot. And he likes to cook. He reckons that this recipe makes the best Irish stew he's ever eaten, which is praise indeed from a Dubliner. I'm quite surprised by this because I make it with supermarket cutlets instead of mutton and King Edward potatoes instead of creamy Irish potatoes. In my version, I leave the carrots in big chunks, add masses of onion and season the stew with plenty of salt, pepper, a sprig or two of thyme and a large quantity of curly parsley to really lift the flavours. The knob of butter added at the end of cooking gives the gravy sheen and body, adding a touch of luxurious creaminess. It is delicious served with hunks of bread and some peas.

1kg/2lb lamb cutlets or lamb shoulder, scrag end
    of neck or chump chops
6 large carrots
6 onions
12 potatoes

6 sprigs thyme
knob cold butter
3 tbsp finely chopped curly parsley
salt and freshly ground black pepper

Trim the bulky fat off the lamb. Peel the carrots and cut each into three – you want big chunks. Peel and quarter the onions, then halve each quarter lengthways. Peel the potatoes and leave to soak in cold water.

Choose a spacious heavy-based flameproof casserole or saucepan with a tight-fitting lid and cover the base with half the chops. Season generously with salt and pepper and half the thyme. Spread half the carrots and onions over the meat. Season again and repeat. Pour 600ml/1 pint water over the stew and bring to the boil. Establish a very low simmer, cover the dish and cook for 40 minutes.

Drain the potatoes, pile over the stew and season thoroughly. Return the lid and cook for another 40 minutes or until the potatoes are tender but firm. Cut the butter into pieces into the stew. Add most of the parsley and gently stir until the butter has dispersed. Sprinkle over the last of the parsley and serve.

Lamb and barley broth

Serves 2–4   *20 minutes preparation: 40 minutes cooking*

This old-fashioned lamb and pearl barley soup-cum-stew smells lip-smackingly good as it simmers away in the background while you get on with something else. The medley of vegetables – yellow swede, orange carrots and bright green peas – and vivacious garnish of parsley, are extremely appetizing. There is plenty here for two meal-sized bowlfuls for two hearty eaters but sufficient quantity for three or four 'normal' ones. Quantities are easy to scale up and the soup reheats perfectly.

1 onion
½ tbsp vegetable oil
2 carrots
1 small swede, about 300g/10oz
375g/12oz shoulder of lamb chops or other stewing
    lamb
50g/2oz pearl barley

½ tsp fresh thyme or ½ tsp dried
1 chicken stock cube dissolved in 750ml/1½ pints
    boiling water
2 spring onions
100g/3½oz frozen peas
1 tbsp chopped parsley
salt and freshly ground black pepper

Peel, halve and finely slice the onion. Heat the oil in a medium-sized, heavy-based saucepan and cook the onion gently, stirring occasionally, while you prepare everything else. Peel the carrots and slice quite thinly. Peel and halve the swede and chop in sugar-lump-sized dice. Trim the lamb of excess fat and skin and cut it into small chunks slightly smaller than you would for kebabs. Wash the pearl barley until the water runs clean.

Stir the meat into the onion, increase the heat and quickly brown it all over. When no red remains, season with ½ teaspoon salt and plenty of pepper. Add the thyme, carrots and swede and stir thoroughly. Cook for a couple of minutes, then add the pearl barley. Now add the stock and bring the soup to the boil. Turn down the heat immediately and skim away the brown foam that will form as best you can; leftovers will soon disperse and won't spoil the flavour of the soup. Partially cover the pan and leave at a low simmer for about 25 minutes or until the pearl barley is puffed (like puffed wheat) and almost tender.

Trim and slice the spring onions. Add the spring onions and peas to the pan, increase the heat slightly and cook, uncovered, for about 5 minutes or until the peas are tender. Taste and adjust the seasoning with salt and pepper. Stir in the parsley and serve.

Burmese lamb and potato curry

Serves 6   *30 minutes preparation: 50–60 minutes cooking*

Over the years, my friend Eddie Lim has often mentioned his Burmese curry. When I eventually tasted it and later cooked it myself – several times – I can see why. It is such a simple recipe. So delicious. And so impressive. The secret of the dish is to cook the onion, garlic and ginger paste until it is dry and beginning to brown, and to seal the meat thoroughly. This results in a rich, thick, rust-coloured, soupy gravy, which is hauntingly subtle but with sufficient chilli heat to make it interesting without blowing your head off. It is worth mentioning that this curry is also very good made with chicken or a mixture of root vegetables with a few green beans or broccoli added at the end. It is served over noodles in deep soup bowls with a garnish of coriander leaves.

6 large garlic cloves
2 large onions
25g/1oz piece fresh ginger
5 scant tbsp olive oil
1 tsp paprika
2 tsp chilli powder
generous pinch of saffron dissolved in 1 tbsp
    boiling water
2 tbsp Thai fish sauce (*nam pla*)

625g/1¼lb casserole lamb or boneless leg
    steaks diced
500g/1lb small waxy potatoes, peeled
1 litre/1¾ pints chicken stock
500g/1lb Chinese or Thai rice noodles
few sprigs coriander
salt

Peel the garlic and onions, and chop the ginger coarsely. Place the ginger and garlic in the bowl of a food processor and blitz. When finely chopped, add the onions and blitz briefly until finely minced.

Heat 3 dessertspoons of the olive oil in a spacious heavy-based saucepan and, when very hot, stir in the onion mixture. Reduce the heat and cook, stirring often, for 20–30 minutes until dry, brown in patches and paste-like. Add the paprika, chilli powder, saffron and fish sauce. Cook, stirring constantly, for 30 seconds. Brown the lamb in uncrowded batches in the rest of the oil in a frying pan. Add the lamb and peeled potatoes to the paste. Add the stock. Bring to the boil, stirring frequently, and simmer for approximately 30 minutes until the meat is tender.

Taste and adjust the seasoning with salt. Five minutes before you are ready to serve, soak the noodles in boiling water. Serve the curry and its soup over the drained noodles and garnish with a few sprigs of coriander. This curry reheats brilliantly.

Lamb provençal

Serves 4   *20 minutes preparation: 35 minutes cooking*

When a dish is described as à la niçoise *or* à la provençale, *it is made with a chunky tomato sauce cooked with garlic, often with onions, and sometimes with olives, anchovies and aubergines. The niçoise version tends to be the more elaborate of the two and might also include capers, artichokes and courgettes. Basil is likely to appear in both and tarragon might be included too. Both sauces are a celebration of local vegetables and flavourings and are liberally interpreted according to what is available. Black olives always appear in niçoise sauces but come and go in provençal versions. Rice is the traditional accompaniment to a provençal dish but new potatoes – boiled first and added at the end of cooking – or green beans and a chunk of bread to mop up the wonderful tomato sauce go very well too. The anchovy, incidentally, is used instead of salt and adds a wonderful depth of flavour which is not the least bit fishy.*

2 onions, about 300g/10oz
3 tbsp olive oil
2 red peppers
1 bay leaf
2 garlic cloves
1kg/2lb lamb fillet
5 large tomatoes, about 625g/1¼lb

1 tsp anchovy essence or 2 canned anchovy fillets
 (optional)
about 20 black olives (optional)
handful basil leaves (optional)
juice ½ lemon
salt and freshly ground black pepper

Peel, halve and finely slice the onions. Add 2 tablespoons of the olive oil to a lidded saucepan that can hold all the ingredients. Stir in the onions, cover the pan and cook over a medium heat for 5 minutes. Meanwhile, use a potato peeler to peel the red peppers. Don't be too finicky about this; you just want to get rid of most of the skin. Cut the peppers into quarters lengthways. Scrape out the seeds and white membrane and slice across the pieces to make strips. Stir the red peppers into the softened onions and cook for 10 minutes, uncovered, adding the bay leaf, and the garlic as soon as you have peeled it and finely sliced in rounds.

While that is going on, trim the lamb fillet and cut into kebab-sized pieces. Place the tomatoes in a bowl of boiling water. Count to 20. Drain the tomatoes, peel and roughly chop. Push the onions and peppers to the side of the pan. Raise the heat and add the remaining olive oil. When very hot, add the meat. Quickly brown it before stirring everything together. Add the anchovy essence or fillets, if using, mashing up the fillets so they dissolve into the sauce, and season with pepper. If not using anchovy, season with salt too.

Add the tomatoes and simmer uncovered for at least 20 minutes until the meat is cooked and the tomatoes have turned into a sauce with the onions and peppers. If it seems too watery, increase the heat to boil off some of the liquid. If including olives and/or basil, add now. Taste the sauce and adjust the seasoning with salt, pepper and lemon juice. This dish reheats well.

Aromatic lamb curry with spinach

Serves 4   *25 minutes preparation: 40 minutes cooking*

If you are a curry novice, this is an excellent recipe to cut your teeth on. I like the fact that it doesn't take hours to cook and that the flavours end up fresh and interesting rather than blowing your head off with fiery heat. It looks pretty too, the thick creamy sauce flecked with chunks of tomato and spinach. Serve it with rice or warm nan bread with a full complement of curry add-ons – poppadoms, lime pickle and raita.

3 large garlic cloves
5cm/2in piece fresh ginger
1 green chilli
5 tbsp Greek yoghurt
1 tsp ground cumin
500g/1lb boneless leg or shoulder lamb steak diced
1 large onion
2 tbsp vegetable oil

1 tsp ground coriander
1 bay leaf
4 cloves
seeds from 4 cardamom pods
200g/7oz young spinach leaves
4 medium tomatoes
generous pinch cayenne or mild paprika
salt

Peel and chop the garlic and ginger. Split the chilli, discard the seeds and chop. Pound these ingredients together to make a paste. Tip the yoghurt into a mixing bowl and whip with half of the ground cumin. Add the paste and meat, stir well, and leave to marinate while you peel and chop the onion.

Heat the vegetable oil in wide pan until very hot. Stir in the onion and cook for a couple of minutes before reducing the heat, sprinkling with ½ teaspoon salt, the remaining cumin, the coriander, bay leaf, cloves and cardamom seeds. Stir thoroughly, cover the pan and cook for 10 minutes until the onion is juicy and lightly coloured.

Meanwhile, bring a large pan of water to the boil, drop in the spinach, return to the boil, cook for 20 seconds, then scoop out of the pan into a colander. Drop the tomatoes into the boiling water, count to 10, remove, then peel and chop. Press the spinach against the side of the colander to drain, then chop. When the onion is ready, increase the heat and add the meat and its yoghurt marinade to the pan. Cook briskly so that the meat browns all over and the yoghurt thickens.

Sprinkle with cayenne or paprika and stir in 200ml/7fl oz boiling water, ½ teaspoon salt and the chopped tomatoes. Bring the curry to the boil, reduce the heat immediately, cover the pan and simmer for 20–30 minutes until the meat is tender. Stir in the spinach, heat through and serve.

Lamb, chickpea and potato hash

Serves 3–4   *20 minutes preparation: 25 minutes cooking*

Comfort food with attitude is how I would describe a bowl of this hash. It is made with the vital ingredients for hash — onions and potatoes — but the protein element, which in this case is minced lamb, comes with layers of interesting extra flavours.

500g/1lb new potatoes
1 large red onion
2 tbsp cooking oil
2 garlic cloves
1 unwaxed lemon
1 tsp thyme leaves
400g/14oz can chickpeas
2 tbsp chopped flat leaf parsley

250g/8oz minced lamb
½ chicken stock cube dissolved in 150ml/¼ pint
   boiling water
1 tbsp chopped mint
Tabasco sauce (optional)
150g/5oz frozen peas
salt and freshly ground black pepper

Put the potatoes on to cook in plenty of salted boiling water until tender. Drain. Return to the pan with cold water to cover and leave for about 30 seconds to cool. Drain again and whip off their skins. Cut the potatoes into chunky wedges by quartering them lengthways.

Meanwhile, halve and thinly slice the red onion. Heat the oil in a large frying pan or large shallow saucepan. Cook the onion until soft and slippery — about 10 minutes. While the onion is cooking, peel and chop the garlic and use a potato peeler or zester to remove the lemon zest in wafer-thin sheets. Chop the zest very finely. Coarsely chop the thyme leaves. Tip the chickpeas into a sieve, rinse well with cold water and shake dry.

Add the garlic, lemon zest, thyme leaves and half the parsley to the pan and stir everything around until the garlic is aromatic. Add the minced lamb and stir-fry until the meat changes colour from pink to brown. Add the stock, the mint, a shake of Tabasco, if you like a hint of chilli zing, and let everything bubble up together for a couple of minutes. Add the chickpeas and juice from half the lemon and the potatoes. Season generously with salt and black pepper and simmer for 10 minutes so the potatoes get a chance to soak up some of the delicious juices and become very hot.

Add the peas and cook for a minute or two until they are tender. Squeeze juice from the remaining lemon half over the top, stir, taste and season again with salt and pepper as necessary. Garnish with the last of the parsley.

Lemon and rosemary lamb with cannellini beans

Serves 2 *20 minutes preparation: 40 minutes cooking*

Lemon zest, garlic and rosemary are a wonderful trinity that often features in Italian cooking. I particularly like it with dried beans – everything chopped small, then fried with a chopped onion before adding the soaked beans – and would recommend it as a way of livening up a can of cannellini or one of the other similar green or white beans. That was the thinking behind this meal-in-a-bowl, which was inspired by the need to use a small amount of meat to good effect without it seeming mean. Being something of a carbohydrate junkie, I like to add boiled new potatoes to dishes like this. You may prefer to leave them out and serve a big bowl of green beans instead.

1 unwaxed lemon	150g/5oz boneless lamb loin
1 large red onion	2 glasses red wine, about 300ml/½ pint
4 large garlic cloves	1 tbsp tomato purée or ketchup
2 tsp rosemary leaves	400g/14oz can cannellini beans
3 tbsp olive oil	2 tbsp parsley
1 bay leaf	salt and freshly ground black pepper

Use a zester or potato peeler to remove four long, wafer-thin strips of zest from the lemon. Tear into small scraps. Peel, halve and finely chop the onion. Peel the garlic and slice in wafer-thin rounds. Very finely chop the rosemary leaves. Heat the olive oil in a medium-sized pan with a heavy base. Add the onion, lemon zest, bay leaf and rosemary, and cook, stirring every now and again, over a medium heat for about 10 minutes until the onion is softening and beginning to brown. Add the garlic and cook for a few more minutes.

Meanwhile, slice the meat into skinny strips, approximately 5 x 1cm/2 x ½in. Clear a space in the middle of the aromatic, browned onion and brown the meat as best you can. Mix the onions into the meat, season generously with salt and pepper and add the red wine and tomato purée or ketchup. Bring to the boil, reduce the heat immediately and then simmer for about 15 minutes.

Meanwhile, tip the cannellini beans into a sieve and rinse under cold running water. Shake dry. Coarsely chop the parsley. Add the beans and half the parsley to the meat and onion. Simmer, crushing the beans slightly with the back of a wooden spoon, and cook for about 10–15 minutes until everything is very hot, the meat cooked through, and the juices are moist but not too wet.

Taste and adjust the seasoning with salt, pepper and lemon juice. Stir in the rest of the parsley. If adding potatoes, cook them separately in salted boiling water and stir them into the stew just before serving.

Moroccan meatballs with peas

Serves 2 *30 minutes preparation: 35 minutes cooking*

If you wanted to eat traditional Moroccan food, as opposed to Frenchified international stuff, at the hotel where I once stayed in Taroudant, it had to be ordered after breakfast. I was determined to try everything, but each meal was so good that every day I was torn between re-ordering what we'd eaten the night before and taking a chance. The bisteeya, *or* pastilla *as it's more commonly known, a flaky, pastry pie stuffed with pigeon and almonds, was so wonderful I nearly asked the kitchen to make one for me to take home. I couldn't resist ordering sweetbreads with preserved lemon and coriander three days running. By comparison, meatballs didn't sound very exciting, but I am so glad we tried them. That night they were made with minced lamb flavoured with cumin and mint, and served in an onion gravy made aromatic with* ras el hanout *(the national spice mix) and sweetened with sultanas and honey. Bobbing in the gravy, adding a fresh lively contrast, were peas and chopped mint. If you cannot find* ras el hanout, *make do with a pinch each of ground mace, cinnamon, nutmeg, cloves, allspice and black pepper.*

2 red onions
1 tbsp cooking oil or half butter and half oil
½ tsp *ras al hanout*
2 tbsp sultanas
½ tbsp runny honey
½ chicken stock cube dissolved in 300ml/½ pint
   boiling water

about 25 mint leaves
250g/8oz minced lamb
½ tsp ground cumin
1 egg yolk
250g/8oz frozen peas
squeeze lemon
salt and freshly ground black pepper

Peel and halve the onions. Finely slice three of the halves. Heat the oil or butter and oil in a deep frying pan or large, shallow saucepan over a high heat. Toss the sliced onions around for a few minutes until beginning to colour. Add the *ras al hanout*, sultanas, honey and 250ml/ 8fl oz of the stock. Bring to the boil, reduce the heat so the liquid simmers, cover the pan and cook for 15 minutes. Remove the lid and cook for a few minutes until the onions are soft, the sultanas plump and the liquid reduced to make a juicy gravy. Salt generously.

Meanwhile, grate the reserved onion half. Chop the mint. Place the lamb in a mixing bowl. Add the grated onion, half the chopped mint, the cumin, a good seasoning of salt and pepper, and the egg yolk. Mix well, mulching together with your hands, forming the mixture into a ball. Rinse your hands, shake dry, then pinch off lumps of the mixture to roll around between your hands to make balls the size of cherry tomatoes. You should end up with about 30 balls.

Add the remaining stock to the gravy, bring back to the boil and add the meatballs. Adjust the heat so the gravy bubbles gently over the balls, allowing them to darken and firm. Roll them around so they cook evenly, add the peas and remaining mint and cook until tender. Taste and adjust the seasoning with salt, pepper and a squeeze of lemon. Serve hot or lukewarm.

Smothered lamb shanks with potatoes

Serves 4   *30 minutes preparation: 60–80 minutes cooking*

Supermarkets have been slow to wake up to our new passion for lamb shanks, a trend kicked off by recipes in the first River Café Cook Book. *When they do sell them, they sell mean, small shanks, so I would suggest you visit a butcher to buy shanks for this recipe. These are the bony end of the leg and you will need one per person for this generous and handsome stew. Don't even think of cutting the thick pad of meat off the bone; not only will the meat taste better on the bone, but it will improve the gravy too. In this dish I've stuck slivers of garlic in the meat and buried the shanks in onions and thyme, adding a few potatoes per person, and covered the lot with water. It needs long, slow cooking over direct heat and can also be cooked in the oven 180°C/350°F/Gas Mark 4. After about an hour, the lamb will be succulent and tender. Serve with carrots and beans.*

4 lamb shanks, on the bone	2 large onions
2 plump garlic cloves	handful thyme sprigs
about 3 tbsp flour	500g/1lb medium potatoes
3 tbsp olive oil	salt and freshly ground black pepper

Trim the lamb shanks, if necessary, of any big flaps of fat. Peel the garlic and slice thinly. Make several slashes in the lamb and post the garlic in the holes. Dust the shanks with flour. Heat 2 tablespoons of the olive oil in a suitable large flameproof casserole and brown the shanks all over, including the ends.

Meanwhile, peel, halve and thinly slice the onions. When the shanks are browned, remove them to a plate. Add the onions to the casserole with the remaining oil. Season with salt and pepper, cover the pan and cook, stirring once or twice, for 5 minutes until the onions are glossy and browned in places. Add the thyme and return the lamb, tucking the pieces, meat side down, into the onions. Add 450ml/¾ pint boiling water and bring the liquid back to the boil.

Meanwhile, peel the potatoes, halve, rinse and tuck them into the dish. Season again with plenty of salt. Bring back to the boil, remove from the heat and lay a double fold of grease-proof paper over the top, tucking it down to touch the food. Add the lid and cook over a medium-low heat for 60 minutes. Check that the meat is meltingly soft. If not, cook for a further 20 minutes or as necessary. Leave to rest for 10 minutes before serving.

Thai salad with lamb

Serves 2–3 *25 minutes preparation: 15 minutes cooking*

If you like spicy food and enjoy clean, fresh flavours with plenty of crunch, then you'll love Thai salads. They make stylish, healthy suppers and once you've armed yourself with a bottle of Thai fish sauce, which is widely available in supermarkets and many late-night stores, you can whip one up in minutes. One good tip is to leave the raw onion in the dressing for a few minutes before the other ingredients are added. This helps to soften it while making it more digestible and less pungent. Despite the fact that Thai salad dressings contain no oil, and no carbohydrates are involved, they are surprisingly satisfying.

2 tbsp lime juice
2 tbsp Thai fish sauce (*nam pla*)
½ tbsp sugar
1 lemon grass stalk
1 small red or green chilli
1 red onion
250g/8oz lamb fillet

1 tbsp vegetable oil
200g/7oz extra fine green beans
½ cucumber
handful mint leaves
handful coriander leaves
2 Little Gem lettuce hearts
salt and freshly ground black pepper

Place the lime juice, fish sauce and sugar in a bowl and stir until the sugar dissolves. Remove the outer leaves of the lemon grass, trim the ends and slice the inner section very finely, cutting on the diagonal. Trim the chilli, split lengthways, scrape out the seeds and slice into tiny strips and then into tiny dice. Stir the lemon grass and chilli into the dressing. Peel the onion, quarter lengthways, then slice down each quarter to make thin slices. Stir the onion into the dressing.

Place a griddle or heavy-based frying-pan over a high heat for several minutes while you prepare the meat. Trim any fat from the meat and smear it with the oil. Season one side with salt and pepper. Lay it, seasoned side down, on the hot griddle, pressing it down with a spatula or fish slice. Cook for 3 minutes. Season the exposed surface and turn the meat. Cook for a further 3 minutes. Turn the meat again, reduce the heat and cook each side for a further couple of minutes. Cook the sides for a couple of minutes each. Turn off the heat and leave the meat for 5 minutes. Transfer to a chopping board and leave to rest while you finish the salad.

Trim and halve the beans. Boil them for 1 minute in salted water, then drain and splash with cold water. Split the cucumber lengthways and use a teaspoon to scrape out the seeds and their watery surrounds. Slice across the halves to make chunky half moons. Stir the beans and cucumber into the dressing with half the coarsely chopped mint and coriander.

Arrange the lettuce leaves on a platter. Lift the salad out of the dressing and scatter over the leaves. Thickly slice the meat and add it and any juices to the salad bowl. Turn the meat through the liquid, then arrange it over the salad. Dribble the rest of the juices over the top. Scatter on the remaining mint and coriander. Serve immediately.

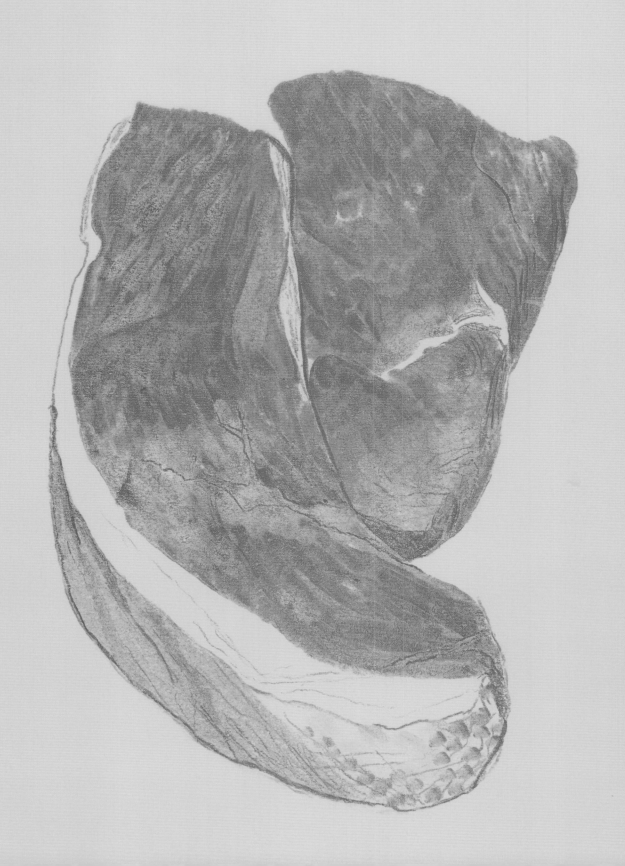

Beef, veal and venison

Nothing beats the flavour and texture of a fine piece of beef. It doesn't matter which cut you choose; as long as it is cooked appropriately, there is nothing comparable. Quickly cooked dishes, like stir-fries and pan-fried recipes, need lean cuts from gently worked muscle like melt-in-the-mouth fillet steak and fat-marbled sirloin steak which embraces entrecote, T-bone and porterhouse steaks. These are all found in the middle of the beast, flanked by the forerib. This is the ultimate joint to roast for flavour and tenderness. Best value for fast cooking are the minute rump steaks and a clutch of shoulder steaks with distinctive ridged meat and curious names like bollo, skirt or *bavette* (the French name) and feather, or the similar French cut called *onglet* which has gristle running down the centre. It's rare to find these cuts in the supermarket, but any butcher worth his salt will be happy to oblige – if he hasn't already nobbled them for his regulars. All these cuts are good for long, slow dishes too, but will be tough if not cooked until the fibres break down and the meat becomes meltingly soft. The fore-quarters of the beast – the shoulders and lower legs, which are the parts that have been worked the hardest – are the best for stewing. These tougher cuts, such as neck, clod, shin, chuck and blade, have plenty of flavour but need long, gentle cooking.

These days, in the wake of BSE and the devastation that followed the outbreak of foot and mouth disease which spread through British beef production, we are all very conscious of the heritage of the meat we eat. We can now buy organic and certifiable beef in the supermarket and are learning to realize that properly reared meat, particularly beef, is never going to be cheap. I don't eat beef that often, and when I do, I buy it from my butcher who specializes in Scottish grass-reared beef.

Venison has become a popular alternative to beef. The meat is very lean, dense-textured, high in protein and low in saturated fat. Treat it like beef, grilling or roasting the loin or saddle and braising the legs. The forequarters can be stewed and are often sold minced. Many people are worried about eating veal because of the cruelty involved to achieve pale meat. It is now possible to buy humanely reared, rosy British veal in the supermarket. My butcher always stocks it and the good news is that British veal is less than half the price of pale Dutch veal.

Chilean beef stew with sweetcorn

Serves 4   *25 minutes preparation: 65 minutes cooking*

Variations on this colourful and interesting stew are plentiful in Chile. Sometimes it's made with lamb and flavoured with ground cumin, while the beef version is usually seasoned with paprika to give it a rich, spicy finish. For a luxurious, creamy gravy, it is sometimes finished with beaten egg stirred into the stew just before it's served.

1 onion
1 bay leaf
2½ tbsp vegetable oil
2 tsp dried oregano
250g/8oz peeled pumpkin
1 leek
2 carrots
400g/14oz beef sirloin or other tender fillet diced

1 tbsp paprika
200g/7oz sweetcorn kernels
500g/1lb small new potatoes
1 chicken stock cube dissolved in 500ml/17fl oz
   boiling water
1 tbsp chopped parsley
salt and freshly ground black pepper

Peel and dice the onion. Place the onion and bay leaf in a spacious heavy-based saucepan with 2 tablespoons of the vegetable oil and stir in the oregano. Cook over a medium heat for 5 minutes while you cut the pumpkin into kebab-sized chunks. Stir the pumpkin into the onion, season with salt and pepper, cover the pan and cook for a further 5 minutes. Trim and slice the leek. Rinse under cold running water and shake dry. Peel the carrots and cut into chunky rounds. Stir the leek and carrots into the onion, cover and cook for a further 5 minutes.

Dust the meat with paprika. Clear the vegetables to the side of the pan, add the remaining oil, increase the heat and add the meat. Brown the meat, then add the sweetcorn, potatoes and chicken stock. Bring to the boil, reduce the heat so the stew simmers steadily, cover the pot and cook for 45 minutes or until the meat is tender. Adjust the seasoning with salt and pepper, stir in the parsley and serve.

A quick and luscious beef stew

Serves 2   *20 minutes preparation: 40 minutes cooking*

This is the perfect recipe for the times when you want the comfort of a good old-fashioned stew but haven't the time to make it properly using one of the more appropriate cuts, such as chuck or shin, that need long, slow cooking. Separately boiled new potatoes – which could be boiled in the pan before you cook the stew – could be added to the pot at the last minute, or you may prefer to eat it with mash over a doorstep of white bread.

3 rashers streaky bacon
1 large onion, about 300g/10oz
2 large field mushrooms
300g/10oz tender, lean frying steak
1 heaped tbsp flour
2 tbsp cooking oil
1 bay leaf
1 glass red wine

1 scant tbsp red currant jelly
½ chicken stock cube dissolved in 350ml/12fl oz
   hot water, or water
3 carrots
100g/3½oz frozen peas
½ tbsp chopped parsley
salt and freshly ground black pepper

Chop the bacon into lardons. Peel and halve the onion, dice one half and slice the other. Slice the mushrooms. Trim the meat and slice it across the grain in thin diagonal strips. Place the meat in a bowl and toss with the flour. Over a low-medium flame, heat half the oil in a heavy-based saucepan that will be able to accommodate all the ingredients. Cook the bacon until beginning to crisp, then add the onion with the bay leaf. After about 5 minutes, when it's starting to look juicy, add the sliced mushrooms and a generous seasoning of salt and pepper. Stir occasionally so the mushrooms cook evenly and, after a few minutes, tip the contents of the pan onto a plate.

Lower the heat, and heat the remaining oil in the pan. Add the meat and all the flour, stirring it around. Cover the pan and leave for 2–3 minutes. Toss the meat and return the lid, making sure the meat is brown and the flour isn't sticking, and cook for a couple more minutes. Remove the lid and add the wine, stirring to scrape up the bits off the bottom of the pan and make a thick gravy. Add the red currant jelly and when it's dissolved add the stock or water. Establish a gentle simmer, then return the onion mixture to the pan and leave to cook very gently for about 15 minutes.

Meanwhile, trim and peel the carrots and slice thinly on the diagonal. Add the carrots to the stew, simmer for 5 minutes, and then add the peas. Cook for a couple more minutes until the peas are tender, check the seasoning and serve sprinkled with parsley.

Catalan veal stew with prunes

Serves 4–6   *30 minutes preparation: 90 minutes cooking*

I don't know about you, but it's not often that I buy red meat on an impulse with no special dish in mind. On one occasion, when there was a particularly long queue at my butcher, I had plenty of time to check out what was on offer. A fine display of various cuts of rosy-pink British veal caught my eye and, as I had vague thoughts of making a stew, I decided on stewing veal.

By chance I came across this bizarre-sounding recipe in a book that I trust implicitly. Patience Gray's Honey From A Week, Fasting and Feasting in Tuscany, Catalonia, The Cyclades and Apulia *is so much more than a cook book. I feel sure everything has been cooked many times and this* estofada, *as they call stews in Catalonia, is exceptional. The prunes, incidentally, are cooked separately and served at one end of a large dish with a mound of fried potatoes at the other. Another odd-seeming ingredient is dark chocolate. Its effect is to thicken the sauce and give it a rich, glossy texture. It's a technique that pops up in some Italian stews and Mexican* mole *and its flavour is virtually imperceptible. I've taken the liberty of slightly adapting the recipe using canned tomatoes and ready-cooked prunes.*

1kg/2lb lean veal	½ tsp paprika
about 4 tbsp olive oil	pinch ground cinnamon
1 large onion	2 sprigs thyme
3 garlic cloves	1 bay leaf
4 canned peeled tomatoes	few sprigs parsley
300ml/½ pint dry white wine	12 large, soft dried prunes
2 tbsp Spanish brandy or whisky	fried potatoes to serve
50g/2oz dark chocolate	salt and freshly ground black pepper

Cut the veal into large kebab-sized chunks. Heat some of the oil in a spacious, heavy-based flameproof casserole and brown the meat in uncrowded batches. Transfer each batch to a plate as you finish.

Peel and slice the onion and brown it in the pan, with the peeled garlic cloves. Crush the tomatoes into the softened onion then add the wine and brandy or whisky. Cook gently for about 15 minutes until the liquid has reduced by about half. Stir in the chocolate together with the paprika and cinnamon. Tie the thyme, bay leaf and parsley in a bundle and add to the pan. Add the meat and its juices and sufficient water just to cover the meat.

Season with salt and pepper and simmer, covered, very gently for 1 hour. Check a piece of meat to see if it is tender; if not, cook for a further 30 minutes or until it is. Simmer the prunes in a little water during the last 15 minutes of cooking. Serve the stew with the prunes and fried potatoes.

Parmesan veal escalopes with rocket salad

Serves 2   *15 minutes preparation: 30 minutes cooking*

The smart way of making escalopes is to do the whole job, the bashing and then the flouring, in greaseproof paper. This eliminates all the mess. The addition of a generous amount of freshly grated Parmesan to the breadcrumbs gives the escalopes extra flavour, making them just that bit more satisfying. I have stipulated veal for this simple but excellent, quick supper, but if you prefer, it would also work brilliantly with turkey or chicken. You can buy turkey escalopes, but you would have to split a chicken breast fillet, opening it out like a book. You should end up with a super-thin piece of meat that has been teased into being double its size rather than battered and torn by too aggressive bashing. The salad is served, restaurant-style, on top of the meat, almost obscuring the escalope. It is one of those useful quick but stylish suppers that is perfect for any occasion and most weathers and is sure to become a favourite mid-week treat. If making the dish for more than two, increase the ingredients in proportion and keep the escalopes warm in a low oven as you finish cooking each one.

50g/2oz bread without crusts
25g/1oz freshly grated Parmesan cheese grated
1 egg
2 veal escalopes
flour for dusting
4 tbsp olive oil

generous knob butter
100g/3½oz cherry tomatoes
50g/2oz rocket
1 tbsp balsamic vinegar
1 lemon (for wedges)
salt and freshly ground black pepper

Blitz the bread to make fine crumbs. Transfer to a large plate or shallow bowl and mix the grated Parmesan into the crumbs. Whisk the egg in a second shallow bowl. Measure off a large double fold of greaseproof paper. Lay one escalope in the middle of one half and fold the other half over the top. Use a rolling pin to bash the escalope gently but firmly until it is the thickness of a coin and more than double its original size.

Dust both sides with flour, shaking away any excess, and repeat the process with the second escalope. Dip the escalopes first in the egg and then in the breadcrumbs and leave to rest while you heat 1 tablespoon of the olive oil and half the butter in a frying pan. When it's hot, lay out one escalope in the pan and cook, adjusting the heat so nothing burns, for about 2 minutes a side until the egg has set, the crumbs turned golden and the meat is cooked through. Transfer to a warmed plate and repeat the process with the second escalope. Quickly quarter the tomatoes. Pile the rocket over the escalopes, scatter over the tomatoes and splash with the balsamic vinegar and remaining olive oil. Season with salt and pepper and serve with lemon wedges.

Corned beef hash with coriander

Serves 2   *15 minutes preparation: 30 minutes cooking*

One unfortunate afternoon, the wife of the owner of my local corner shop in west London was alone behind the counter when half a dozen unfamiliar youths came into the premises. Within minutes they had taken up strategic positions and she was powerless to stop a couple of them going upstairs to pilfer from her home. Fortunately there was no physical damage, but the shock was so great that the shop has closed. It was a useful place for basic stuff such as potatoes, onions, corned beef and tomatoes, which are necessary for this comforting childhood fry-up. I got the idea of jazzing up the hash with Indian seasonings from my corner shop and, despite the depressing legacy now attached to the dish, it's such a good twist on an old favourite, that I want to pass on the details. To add a healthy note, serve the hash with steamed spinach.

500g/1lb potatoes	½ tsp ground coriander
3 shallots	100g/3½oz corned beef
1 small chilli	2 plum tomatoes
5cm/2in piece fresh ginger	1 tbsp chopped fresh coriander
1 garlic clove	2 large eggs
3 tbsp vegetable oil	salt and freshly ground black pepper
½ tsp ground turmeric	

Boil the potatoes in plenty of salted for about 15 minutes until tender. Place the pan under the cold tap and let it run for a couple of minutes. Drain and peel the potatoes, then cut into dice about the size of sugar lumps.

Meanwhile, peel and finely chop the shallots. Trim and split the chillis, scraping away the seeds. Slice into skinny strips and then into tiny dice. Peel the ginger and grate or finely chop. Peel and finely chop the garlic. Heat 1 tablespoon of the oil in a large frying pan and stir in the shallots, chilli and garlic. Cook for about 5 minutes over a medium heat until the shallots are beginning to soften. Stir in the turmeric and ground coriander, cook for a few more seconds, then squash the shallots against the side of the pan, add another tablespoon of oil, turn up the heat and add the potatoes. Scoop the shallots over the potatoes and cook for 5 minutes over a brisk heat.

Chunk the corned beef or crumble it coarsely if using ready-cut slices. Core the tomatoes then chop quite small. Add the corned beef, tomatoes and half the fresh coriander to the pan. Season generously with salt and pepper. Stir and leave to cook for 5 minutes. Scoop up the bottom layer and cook for a further 10 minutes. Divide the hash between two hot plates. Add the remaining oil to the pan and quickly fry the eggs. Place an egg on top of each plate of hash and sprinkle with the last of the fresh coriander.

Albondigas wrap with cherry tomatoes and lettuce hearts

Serves 4   *15 minutes preparation: 20 minutes cooking*

On my first night in Barcelona I played Russian roulette at Cerveceria Catalana, one of this city's best tapas bars. Picking from a plate of deep fried little chillies called padrane, *I munched my way through half a dozen before I was hit by the explosive buzz. Recovery was quick thanks to other delicious morsels such as wafers of tomato-rubbed toast piled high with slippery salt cod with a smear of sweet tomato purée and pungent Serrano ham with roasted red pepper. I would grow very fat if I lived near this wonderful place. It is easy, for example, to spear through a bowl of* albondigas, *the herby miniature meatballs so beloved of tapas bars. They go well with spaghetti and a quick tomato sauce made by grilling then blitzing cherry tomatoes, but I like them piled into warm pitta bread envelopes with soft cherry tomatoes and crunchy lettuce hearts.*

500g/1lb cherry tomatoes
4 tbsp olive oil
1 tbsp balsamic vinegar
50g/2oz white bread, without crusts
1 plump garlic clove
2 tbsp milk or 1 tbsp cream or thick Greek yoghurt
1 onion
500g/1lb minced beef
3 tbsp finely chopped flat leaf parsley

½ tsp fresh thyme
generous pinch nutmeg, preferably freshly grated
1 egg
2 tbsp flour
4 tbsp dry sherry, preferably Oloroso
4 Little Gem lettuce hearts
4 pitta breads
salt and freshly ground back pepper

Put the tomatoes, 2 tablespoons of the olive oil and the balsamic vinegar in a frying pan and cook, shaking the pan occasionally, for 10–15 minutes until the tomatoes are soft and squashy but keeping their shape. Tip into a bowl to cool. Place the bread and peeled garlic clove in the bowl of a food processor and blitz into fine crumbs. Stir in the milk, cream or yoghurt.

Peel, halve and finely chop the onion. Add it to the food processor bowl with the meat, 2 tablespoons of the parsley, the thyme, nutmeg, ½ teaspoon salt and a generous grating of black pepper. Beat the egg and then blitz in a few short bursts, until thoroughly blended and combined. Rinse your hands in cold water, then pinch off small lumps and roll between your hands into cherry-tomato-sized balls.

Dust the meatballs with flour. Heat the remaining oil in the (cleaned) frying pan over a medium heat and fry the meatballs in batches, turning so they brown all over and cook through. Allow about 10 minutes per batch. Remove them from the pan, pour in the sherry and allow to bubble up and reduce to a sticky syrup. Return the meatballs and roll in the juices. Sprinkle on the remaining parsley, trim and quarter the lettuce hearts, then shred lengthways. Warm the pittas in the toaster, split down one side and fill with meatballs, tomatoes and lettuce. Eat at once.

Italian venison stew with Marsala

Serves 4–6   *30 minutes preparation: 90 minutes cooking*

The Italians have a lovely way of livening up the look and taste of stewed dishes with finely chopped parsley, lemon zest and garlic. They call this fiesty seasoning gremolata *or* gremolada *and it works a treat with this interestingly gamey venison stew. In Italy it would be served with buttery polenta rather than mashed potato. I like it with plenty of crusty bread such as ciabatta. As always with stews, flavours mature if the dish is left overnight and reheated the next day.*

75g/3oz chopped pancetta or rindless smoked
   streaky bacon
2 onions
3 garlic cloves
1 large sprig rosemary
50g/2oz butter
3 tbsp olive oil
1kg/2lb venison stewing steak, cut into large pieces
100ml/3½fl oz red wine vinegar
150ml/¼ pint red wine

2 chicken stock cubes
1 bay leaf
½ tsp ground cloves
10 juniper berries
½ tsp ground allspice
3 tbsp flour
1 small glass Marsala
small bunch flat leaf parsley
1 large unwaxed lemon
salt and freshly ground black pepper

Finely chop the pancetta or bacon. Peel, halve and finely chop the onions. Peel the garlic and chop 2 cloves finely. Strip the leaves from the sprig of rosemary and chop very finely.

Heat half the butter and the oil in a large, heavy-based saucepan and stir in the pancetta, onions, garlic and rosemary. Cook, stirring often, for 10 minutes until the onions are browned and the pancetta crisp. Increase the heat and add the venison. Brown the meat very thoroughly all over, then season generously with salt and pepper. Now add the vinegar, letting it cook into the meat while loosening the sticky brown goo at the bottom of the pan. Add the wine, let it bubble up and cook for several minutes until reduced to a syrup. Dissolve the stock cubes in 1 litre/1¾ pints boiling water and add half of it to the pan. Add the bay leaf, cloves, juniper berries and ground allspice. Return the liquid to a simmer, cover the pan and cook for 1 hour.

Melt the remaining butter in a small pan and stir in the flour to make a smooth, thick paste. Gradually add the remaining stock, stirring as it comes up to the boil, to make a smooth, thick sauce. Simmer for a couple of minutes then add to the stew. Return the stew to the boil, add the Marsala, reduce the heat to a simmer and cook for 20 minutes or until the meat is quite tender. Taste and adjust the seasoning with salt and pepper.

Strip the parsley leaves from the stalks. Use a zester or potato peeler to remove the lemon zest in paper-thin sheets. Finely chop the parsley and lemon zest and the remaining garlic clove. Now chop all three together. Serve the stew with a sprinkling of the *gremolata*.

Picadillo with coconut chilli rice

Serves 4   *15 minutes cooking: 35 minutes cooking*

Cooking minced beef with raisins, green olives, capers, tomatoes and sweet peppers might sound odd but just you try it. The result is an interesting flavour with nuggets of sweet and sour. In Chile they serve it with rice and call it picadillo, *in Mexico they top it with cornmeal (polenta) and call it* tamale *pie and in the West Indies they spread it on mashed breadfruit, roll it up like a Swiss roll and call it breadfruit sandwich. The exact proportion of sweet/sour ingredients is a matter of taste, but this is an occasion when more is better than less. Rum punch would go very well with this.*

1 onion
1 red or green pepper or 3 celery sticks
2 tbsp vegetable or sunflower oil
4 large garlic cloves
zest 1 lime
1 small red or green chilli
300g/10oz basmati rice
200ml/7fl oz carton coconut cream or canned coconut milk
500g/1lb good-quality minced beef
100g/3½oz green olives

400g/14oz passata or liquidized can peeled tomatoes
2 tbsp raisins, preferably Spanish, Italian or Australian (bigger, juicier and sweeter)
2 tbsp capers
1 glass white wine, about 150ml/¼ pint
Angostura bitters (optional)
2 tbsp chopped flat leaf parsley or coriander
avocado slices and lime wedges to serve
salt and freshly ground black pepper

Peel and finely chop the onion. Finely chop the pepper, discarding the stalk, seeds and white membrane. If using celery, dice or slice thinly. Fry the onion and chopped pepper or celery in the oil in a spacious frying pan or similarly wide-based saucepan. Stir a couple of times and cook for about 6 minutes until the onion is beginning to colour.

Meanwhile, peel and finely chop the garlic. Use a zester or potato peeler to remove the lime zest in paper-thin sheets. Trim and split the chilli, scrape away the seeds and chop finely. Place the rice in a saucepan with the coconut milk, lime zest and chilli. Add 100ml/3½fl oz water. Bring to the boil, turn down the heat to very low, clamp on the lid and cook for 15 minutes. Leave, without removing the lid, for at least 5 minutes.

Add the meat to the onion, increase the heat and fry, breaking up the lumps, for about 5 minutes. Add the next 5 ingredients plus a generous seasoning of salt and pepper. Stir well. Turn down the heat and simmer for 25–30 minutes until the sauce is thick but still wet. Taste and adjust the seasoning with salt, pepper, a squeeze of lime juice and Angostura bitters if you have some.

Remove the lime zest from the rice. Serve the rice and picadillo together, garnished with the parsley or coriander, giving each serving 2 or 3 slices of avocado and a wedge of lime.

Indian venison burgers with cucumber raita

Serves 2   *15 minutes preparation: 20 minutes cooking*

Minced venison is a lean healthy option that is immensely versatile. Turn it into meatballs, for example, served, perhaps, in a plum, gin and juniper sauce, as they do with the haunch of deer at Rules, an old-fashioned British restaurant in London's Covent Garden. Indian restaurants are very keen on venison and that is where the inspiration came from for these exceptionally delicious little burgers. I serve them with nan bread, which puffs and swells like pitta bread in a hot oven and is the perfect envelope to hold the burgers. A good accompaniment is home-made raita, which is turned into a full-scale salad by adding plenty of big chunks of cucumber.

100g/3½oz shallots or red onion	1 tomato
2 tbsp vegetable oil	½ cucumber
1 small green chilli	1 garlic clove
1 tsp ground cumin	300g/10oz natural yoghurt
1 tsp ground coriander	1 tbsp olive oil
½ tsp ground turmeric	squeeze lemon juice
4 tbsp chopped fresh coriander	2 peshwari nan
2 venison grill steaks or 375g/12oz minced venison	salt

Peel, halve and finely chop the shallots or onion. Gently fry the shallots or onion in 1 tablespoon of the oil for several minutes until softened without much colouring. Meanwhile, split the chilli, scrape away the seeds, slice into skinny batons and across into tiny scraps. Add the chilli, cumin, coriander and turmeric to the pan, stir and cook for about a minute before tipping the mixture into a mixing bowl.

Add 2 tablespoons of the chopped fresh coriander and the venison to the bowl and use your hands to mix and mulch thoroughly. Divide the mixture into four and form into even-sized patties. Wipe out the frying pan, add the remaining oil and, when hot, fry the burgers over a medium heat for 5 minutes a side, then reduce the heat and cook for a further 3 minutes a side or until cooked through.

Meanwhile, make the raita. Dice the tomato. Split the cucumber and use a teaspoon to remove the seeds. Chop into small chunks. Peel and chop the garlic and crush to a paste with a little salt. Mix the garlic paste, olive oil and lemon juice into the yoghurt. Add the tomato, cucumber chunks and the remaining chopped coriander. If convenient, preheat the oven to 200°C/400°F/Gas Mark 6 and heat up the nan. When they are puffed, halve the nan and serve the burgers and raita in the bread. Alternatively, warm the bread on a griddle.

New York steak salad with horseradish

Serves 2   *15 minutes preparation: 10–15 minutes cooking*

This salad takes a leaf out of the Thai salad book. Theirs are packed with interesting textures and flavours and are usually a mix of hot and cold, cooked and raw, spicy and sweet flavours. There is none of the characteristic chilli heat in this salad, but the crunch of tiny scraps of red onion mingling with lightly cooked runner beans – the sort which have been sliced long and thin and end up looking like green spaghetti – wakens up the taste buds. Cherry tomatoes add a sweetness that lifts the flavours and provides a counterbalance to the creamy, horseradish-spiked salad dressing. This interesting mix of flavours goes well with steak, and when the steak is served Thai-salad-style in thinly sliced strips, it brings a touch of fashionable fusion presentation to a relatively straightforward dish.

375g/12oz thick sirloin steak
2 tbsp olive oil
300g/10oz stringless runner beans, long cut
100g/3½oz cherry tomatoes
1 small red onion

1 tbsp mayonnaise
½ tbsp red wine vinegar
½ tbsp creamed horseradish
1 tbsp chopped flat leaf parsley
salt and freshly ground black pepper

Smear the steak on both sides with slightly less than half the olive oil. Heat a ridged grill pan (or frying pan) for several minutes until very hot. Season one side of the steak with salt and pepper and lay it, seasoned side down, in the pan. Use tongs or a fish slice to press the steak down for maximum initial contact and cook for a couple of minutes until you see the contact meat turning brown and crusty. Season the uncooked surface, turn and repeat. Depending on the thickness of the steak, this timing will produce a rare steak. If you like it cooked medium, turn the steaks again, cooking for a further minute on each side. Lift the steak onto a chopping board and leave for several minutes to relax.

Meanwhile, make the salad. Drop the beans into a large pan of salted boiling water and boil for 3 minutes. Drain carefully in a colander, shaking it several times. Halve the tomatoes through their middles, or lengthways if plum cherry tomatoes. Peel, halve and finely chop the onion. Spoon the mayonnaise into a mixing bowl, stir in the vinegar, then the creamed horseradish and finally gradually beat in the remaining olive oil. Stir the chopped onion into the dressing. Add the beans, tomatoes and parsley. Season lightly with salt and generously with black pepper and toss thoroughly.

Divide the salad between two plates. Trim any fat from the steak, then slice thinly across the width, cutting slightly at a slant. Drape the steak over the salad and dribble the juices over the top. Eat now or later.

Smoked chili con carne with cherry tomatoes

Serves 4   *30 minutes preparation: 60 minutes cooking*

One of my favourite ingredients is 'soft' La Chinata smoked paprika from the Extremadura region of Spain. Locally grown capsicums are dried over oak-wood fires to make a brick-red powder giving the otherwise mild and gentle paprika a distinctive smoky taste. I've used it in all sorts of dishes, but when combined with chilli powder, cumin and oregano, it gives this version of chili con carne a rich and robust flavour that completely alters the dish. Another surprise addition is cherry tomatoes. These are added at the end of cooking and cook to a seductive melting consistency which injects a fresh, sweet acidity into most mouthfuls. The chilli heat is perfect for me; if you want to blow your head off rather than enjoy the subtlety of the dish, tune it up with Tabasco. Serve it over a mound of steaming rice.

4 rindless rashers smoked streaky bacon
3 tbsp vegetable oil
2 onions
2 large garlic cloves
1 small unwaxed lemon
750g/1½lb lean beef
2 heaped tsp smoked paprika
1 heaped tsp each chilli powder, ground cumin
   and dried oregano
½ tbsp flour

2 glasses red wine
200g/7oz canned chopped tomatoes
1 chicken stock cube dissolved in 500ml/17fl oz
   hot water
1 bay leaf
250g/8oz cherry tomatoes
400g/14oz can red kidney beans
150ml/¼ pint soured cream
small bunch chives
salt

Cut the bacon across the rashers into strips. Heat 1 tablespoon of the oil in a frying pan. Cook bacon, gently at first, until crisp. Scoop it out onto a large plate. Meanwhile, peel and chop the onions and garlic. Cook both in the bacon oil, adding a big pinch of salt, for about 6 minutes until slippery and lightly browned. Remove the zest from half the lemon and shred or cut into scraps. Stir zest into the onion; cook for two minutes. Tip the onion mixture into the bacon.

Chop the beef into pieces about half the size of kebab chunks. Using the rest of the oil, brown the meat in batches in the frying pan, so it gets crusty rather than juicy, transferring the batches to a plate as you go. Return all the meat to the pan. Sprinkle the paprika, chilli, cumin, oregano and 1 teaspoon salt over the meat, stir well and cook for a couple of minutes before stirring in the flour. Cook for a minute or so.

Add the wine, stir well and cook over a medium heat for 5–10 minutes until reduced by half. Add the canned tomatoes, stock and bay leaf. Simmer steadily, uncovered, over a medium heat for 30 minutes until the meat is tender and the liquid reduced. Taste and adjust the seasoning with salt and lemon juice. Add the cherry tomatoes and simmer for 5 minutes. Tip the beans into a sieve, rinse with cold water and shake dry. Add the beans to the pan. Cook for a further 5 minutes. Serve with a dollop of soured cream and garnish of snipped chives.

Spag bol Florentine

Serves 4–6   *15 minutes preparation: 60 minutes cooking*

Thick, terracotta-brown and rich with flavour. The Florentine bit refers to spinach. This gives the sauce a splash of colour and you your greens, but you can leave it out if you like. Ragu *improves if it is left overnight. Serve with spaghetti or your favourite pasta. It is also good rolled up in blanched cabbage leaves with a chunky tomato sauce, in wraps and for making 'instant' lasagne with soak-and-go lasagne squares.*

4 rindless rashers streaky bacon
50g/2oz butter
1 tbsp cooking oil
1 onion
2 carrots
2 celery sticks
450g/14½oz minced beef
1 large glass red wine or ½ chicken stock cube
    dissolved in 250ml/8fl oz hot water

150ml/¼ pint milk
¼ tsp grated nutmeg, 2–3 gratings if using whole
    nutmeg
250ml/8fl oz passata (or 400g/14oz can whole
    tomatoes, puréed and sieved)
squeeze lemon juice
100g/3½oz young leaf spinach
salt and freshly ground black pepper

Dice the bacon. Heat half the butter and the oil in a heavy-based pan over a medium heat and fry the bacon until crisp. Remove from the pan. Meanwhile, peel and finely chop the onion and the carrots. Trim and peel the celery and finely chop (including the leaves, if there are any). Add the onion to the pan and fry for a couple of minutes before adding the carrots and celery. Cook for 5 minutes, stirring a couple of times, then add the meat.

Stir as it changes from pink to brown. Season generously with salt. Add the wine or stock and increase the heat to medium-high. Cook, stirring occasionally, until all the wine has evaporated. Add the milk and nutmeg. Continue to cook, stirring frequently, and when the milk has almost entirely disappeared (it takes about 10 minutes) add the passata. Return the bacon to the pan. Cook at a gentle simmer, uncovered, for 45 minutes.

Taste the *ragu*, adjusting the seasoning with salt, pepper and a squeeze of lemon juice. Cook uncovered for at least 15 minutes until thick and moist rather than wet. Stir the spinach into the *ragu* and cook for about 5 minutes until wilted and integrated into the sauce. Stir in the remaining butter and serve.

Thai beef salad with grapes

Serves 4   *20 minutes preparation: 10 minutes cooking*

*Thai salads are perfect if you're trying to shed pounds because they contain hardly any oil.
Instead, the dressing is sweet and sour, pungent and as chilli hot as you like. Any Thai beef
salad I've ever eaten has been made with quickly seared beef that is crusty on the outside but
pink within. Don't bother with this salad unless you chose a decent piece of steak, because it
must be very tender. It's the crunchy vegetables that should exercise your jaws. The sweetness
from the grapes is a lovely fresh surprise. There is plenty here for four big eaters, but a bowl of
hot new potatoes tossed with mint would be a lovely accompaniment.*

200g/7oz green beans	½ cucumber
1 large garlic clove	1 celery heart
1–2 small red chillies	15g/½oz bunch coriander
2 tbsp Thai fish sauce (*nam pla*)	100g/3½oz seedless red grapes
½ tbsp brown sugar	1 large rump steak, about 375g/12oz
½ tbsp soy sauce or oyster sauce	1 tbsp cooking oil
2 limes	15g/½oz bunch mint
2 red onions	salt and freshly ground black pepper

Put a large pan of salted water on to boil. Top and tail the beans and cut them in half. Add
the beans to the boiling water. Cook for 2 minutes, drain and splash with cold water to cool.
Peel and finely chop the garlic. Sprinkle with a little salt and work to a paste. Split the chilli
or chillies, scrape away the seeds, slice into skinny batons, then chop into tiny dice. Place the
garlic and chilli in a salad bowl. Add the fish sauce, brown sugar, soy or oyster sauce and juice
of the limes. Stir well. Peel, halve and finely slice the onions, cutting down rather than across
the halves. Stir the onions into the dressing; after a few minutes they will wilt slightly.

Peel the cucumber, split it lengthways and scrape out the seeds and their watery surround.
Slice the cucumber into half moons. Trim the celery heart and peel the outer stalks if they
look stringy. Slice across the heart as finely as you can. Tip into a colander and rinse under
cold running water. Shake dry. Place the cucumber and celery on top of the onions. Coarsely
chop the coriander leaves and halve the grapes. Add both to the salad.

To cook the steak, heat a griddle (or frying pan) until very hot. Rub the steak with cooking oil
and season one side with salt and pepper. Slap the seasoned side down onto the griddle and
press it down hard with a fish slice, holding it there for 1 minute. Season the exposed side
with salt and pepper, turn the steak and repeat. Depending on the thickness of the steak and
how rare you like it, either remove the steak to rest or repeat the cooking on each side. Allow
the steak to sit for 5 minutes before seasoning again and slice very thinly. Toss the salad, add
the steak and any juices and toss again. Coarsely chop the mint and scatter over the top. Eat.

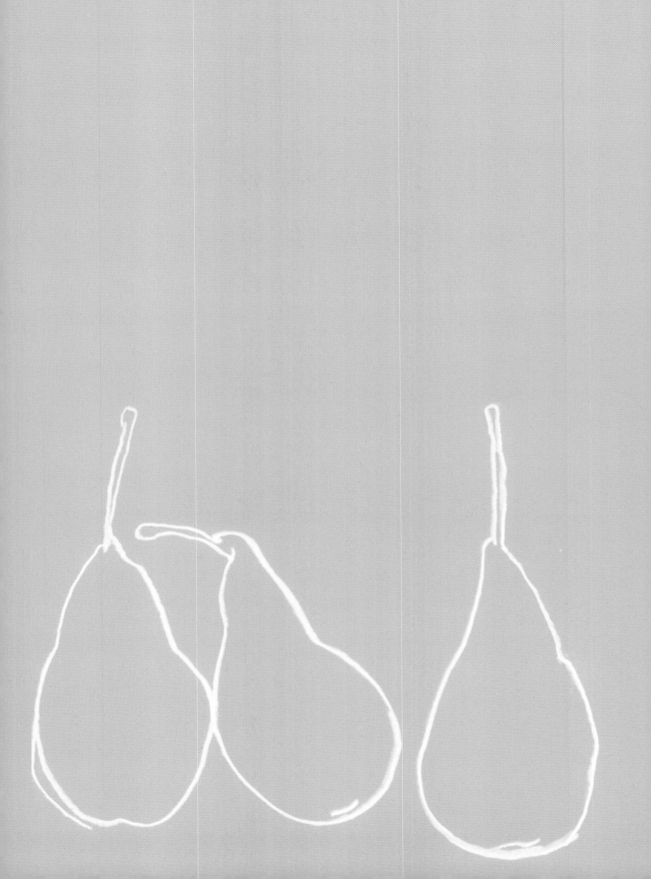

Puddings

One of my best friends is what I'd call a puddaholic. In my restaurant-reviewing days, we once went to Langan's Brasserie and had a four-course meal entirely of puddings. We started with raspberries and vanilla ice cream, followed with rice pudding (with strawberry jam), went on to treacle tart and finished with something very dark and intensely chocolaty. Throughout our 'meal' we drank champagne. I can't say I'd rush to repeat the experience, but I do like to finish a meal with something sweet. At home, I'm usually on the look-out for something quick and easy to make and I either want a fresh and light pudding or a gorgeous bowl of stodge to sink my spoon into. I am particularly fond of rice puddings and include here four very different ones, all of which can be cooked over direct heat. This sort of filling pudding suits the times when my sweet tooth kicks in and it becomes the main part of the meal. As before, all these recipes are cooked or prepared in one pan and are served in a bowl rather than on a plate.

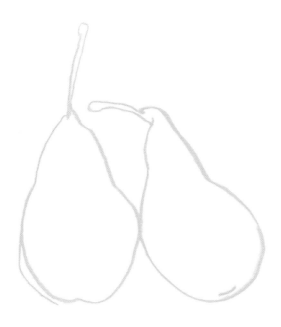

Moroccan rice pudding

Serves 6   *15 minutes preparation: 30 minutes cooking*

When rice pudding is mentioned, anyone brought up in Britain knows what you're talking about. It either comes out of a tin and is very sweet and creamy, or it has been baked in the oven until the milk forms a floppy brown skin. Both are bland and traditionally served in large portions. There are those among us who love both types, especially when it is eaten with a dusting of caster sugar, a dollop of thick cream and a scoop of strawberry jam. Moroccan rice pudding is quite different.

In Morocco, the milk they use is often flavoured with ground almonds and the pudding is cooked with cinnamon and only a hint of sugar. Like us they use round-grain 'pudding' rice, but it is cooked slowly in a saucepan until the rice swells with absorbed milk and clings together in a loose creamy sauce. A knob of butter or, in my adaptation, a scoop of cream, combines with a slug of orange-flower water to point up the flavours. The perfect contrast is a garnish of toasted almonds and pistachios.

50g/2oz ground almonds
600ml/1 pint milk
1 cinnamon stick
5cm/2in strip orange zest
1 vanilla pod
150g/5oz pudding rice
50g/2oz unrefined organic cane sugar
3 tbsp orange-flower water
4 tbsp double cream

small knob butter
2 tbsp shredded almonds
handful skinned pistachio nuts
cinnamon for dusting
sliced oranges dusted with icing sugar and
    cinnamon, and thick cream or Greek yoghurt to
    serve (optional)
salt

Place the ground almonds in a medium-sized saucepan with 250ml/8fl oz boiling water. Boil for 2 minutes, then add the milk, cinnamon stick, orange zest, vanilla pod and a pinch of salt. Bring to boiling point while stirring constantly, turn down the heat and simmer for 5 minutes.

Add the rice to the pan. Simmer very gently, stirring occasionally, for about 20 minutes or until the rice is tender and most of the liquid absorbed. Stir in the sugar. Add the orange-flower water and 2 tablespoons of the double cream and cook for 1 more minute until thick but sloppy. Leave to cool in the pan. When tepid, remove the cinnamon stick and vanilla pod (both can be wiped and re-used) and break up the orange zest into little scraps. Stir in the rest of the cream.

Transfer to a serving bowl. Melt the knob of butter in a frying pan, add the shredded almonds and toss until golden. Drain on absorbent kitchen paper and use to garnish the rice pudding. Roughly chop the pistachios and add them too. Dust with cinnamon and, if liked, serve with sliced oranges dusted with icing sugar and cinnamon, and thick cream or Greek yoghurt.

Cranachan

Serves 6   *10 minutes preparation: 5 minutes cooking*

A plate of perfect raspberries lightly dusted with caster sugar and served with home-made vanilla ice cream is, for me, a Desert Island dessert. The finest raspberries come from Scotland and the Scots have a delicious tradition of combining them with whisky-whipped cream and toasted oatmeal. I give here the basic recipe for Cranachan, but it is one of those dishes that is open to interpretation: more whisky, more sugar, more raspberries or more crunchy oats. Whatever. Suit yourself. Get in the swing of things by serving it with shortbread biscuits and a wee dram.

50g/2oz jumbo or ordinary porridge oats
300ml/½ pint whipping cream
2 tbsp runny honey or icing sugar

3 tbsp whisky
400g/14oz ripe raspberries

Sprinkle the oats over a wide, heavy-based pan such as a roasting tray or large frying pan and place over a moderate heat, shaking occasionally, until toasted and golden. Remove from the pan to cool.

Pour the cream into a mixing bowl and whip with the honey or sifted icing sugar until it begins to form peaks. Fold in the whisky, then three-quarters of the raspberries and three-quarters of the toasted oats.

Divide the mixture between six glass bowls or transfer to a suitable serving bowl. Garnish with the remaining raspberries and oats. Dust with a little more icing sugar or with a dribble of whisky. Chill and serve.

Eton mess

Serves 6 *20 minutes preparation*

Some dishes manage to become familiar without anyone knowing exactly what they are. Eton mess, for example, which is another name for strawberry fool, links the name of a famous public school with disorder or the army slang for a meal, and is immediately attractive and very familiar. Most people have heard of it and occasionally it pops up on restaurant menus, in magazines and cook books, and the common denominator is strawberries and cream, although no two recipes are the same. At Eton, apparently, a 'mess' means taking tea in your room with 'a mess' of one or two other boys. One friend remembered a banana mess of mashed banana with two scoops of ice cream and loads of cream, and thought the strawberry version something that might be served at the 4th June College picnic, held every year to celebrate the birthday of King George III. It is not surprising that the half dozen or so Old Etonians I consulted had never eaten Eton mess, because the College chef confirmed that it hasn't been on the menu for years. Fortunately, because it's a great dish, their librarian dug out the Eton College recipe, dated 1936, and mentioned the name Pellaprat, a famous French chef who is regarded with the same reverence as Escoffier. It seems likely that he invented the dish when a load of over-ripe strawberries needed eating up. His disguise was a fluff of whipped cream and the fool was served with sponge fingers. Somewhere along the line, someone else had the idea of stirring chunks of meringue into the fool at the last moment. If you make your own meringues or buy good-quality ones, they give it delicious bursts of sweet, light crunch with a slight chew.

750g/1½lb very ripe English strawberries
2 tbsp caster sugar

400g/14oz whipping cream
12 mini meringues

Quickly rinse the strawberries under cold running water and shake dry. Remove the stalks – the neatest way to do this is with a small, sharp knife, cutting at an angle around and under the stalk, to remove a small cone, turning the strawberry rather than the knife. Leave small strawberries whole, halve medium ones and quarter large fruit. Place the fruit in a bowl, sprinkle over the sugar and leave to melt and turn the strawberries juicy. Toss and leave for at least 10 minutes.

Whip the cream in the bowl in which you intend serving the fool, until it is thick, fluffy and holds soft peaks. Drain the juices from the strawberries into the cream. Give a quick stir and then add the strawberries. Stir, crushing some of the strawberries as you mix. Quarter the meringues and loosely fold them into the cream.

If you prefer, hold back half the strawberries, then pass them through a sieve directly into the fool, stirring to get swirls of seed-free strawberry purée.

Green fruit salad with avocado cream

Serves 4   *20 minutes preparation*

Kiwi fruit was first introduced into the UK in 1953 and remained something of a mystery until the seventies when it became a cliché of nouvelle cuisine, or small food on big plates as it was known. Slices of its green pulp with distinctive black seeds adorned everything from fruit salads and gateaux to fans of duck breast with raspberry coulis. When someone discovered the high vitamin C content of kiwi fruit – ten times more than the equal weight of a lemon – it caught on in a minor way as a health food. It's useful, too, in the fruit bowl, because it keeps well and brings a bit of unexpected colour to fruit salads. Baby kiwi are about the same size as a large cherry tomato and their shiny, smooth skin is dark green. Unlike normal kiwi, which often need a few days in a warm kitchen before they are ready to eat, baby kiwi are sold ripe and ready to eat. They will appeal to anyone who likes sweet fruit and for my taste they work best in a salad with plenty of acidity to counterbalance their sweetness. I came across avocado cream in Spain, but think the idea probably originated in Brazil. It's a lovely dessert in its own right, but goes very well with this green fruit salad.

125g/4oz kiwi fruit (use baby ones if you can
   find them)
200g/7oz white grapes
4 ripe Conference pears
5 tbsp lime juice

2 oranges
4 passion fruit
2 ripe avocados
4 tbsp caster sugar

Peel the baby kiwi, then slice them in two or three rounds and transfer to a mixing bowl. Halve or quarter the grapes lengthways depending on their size. Remove the stalks from the pears and quarter them lengthways. Cut out the core and cut into dice about the size of a sugar lump. Scoop the grapes and pear into the bowl and add 1 tablespoon of lime juice. Halve the oranges and squeeze the juice over the fruit salad. Toss everything together. Halve the passion fruit and scrape the contents of the shell over the top.

Run a sharp knife round the avocados and twist apart. Discard the stone and use a spoon to scrape the flesh into a small bowl. Add the remaining lime juice and the sugar and use a fork to mash and mix everything together, stirring to make a smooth, thick, green cream. Taste and adjust the seasoning with extra lime juice or sugar.

Place a scoop of the avocado cream in the middle of four serving dishes. Spoon over the fruit salad, making sure each serving has a decent share of passion fruit.

Poached pears with lemon and lavender

Serves 6   *15 minutes preparation: 30 minutes cooking*

People used to make a special detour to see the lavender bush that flourished outside my mother's house on Chislehurst Common in Kent. Each year it grew bigger and more spectacular, echoing the stupendous bushes, nay fields of bushes, of purple lavender that grow around Grasse in the south of France. As far as I can recall, it was never used for cooking, although its aromatic fragrance always reminded me of rosemary and still makes me think of roast lamb. Although I've not seen lavender on sale in a food shop, it is easy enough to come by from gardens. Flower heads lend a subtle and haunting elegance to all sorts of dishes and work wonderfully well in pears poached in white wine sweetened with honey and lifted by lemon zest. Poached pears are always a lovely dessert at any time of the year. I like them cold, served standing in the reduced juices of their poaching liquid, and would suggest accompanying them with crème fraîche or good-quality vanilla ice cream that is softened slightly more than is usual. Pinot gris, incidentally, is the grape variety used in Alsace wines. Any white wine would work in this recipe, although I would avoid anything very sweet.

6 lavender stalks
about 600ml/1 pint Alsace white wine
2 scant tbsp runny honey or sugar

1 unwaxed lemon
6 even-sized Conference pears
6 tbsp crème fraîche

Place the lavender flowerheads in a pan that can hold the pears comfortably in a single layer. Add the wine and honey or sugar. Remove 2 paper-thin strips of zest from the lemon. Add them to the pan. Place the pan over a medium-low heat and gently bring to the boil, swirling the pan a few times until the sugar dissolves or the honey melts. Boil the liquid hard for a couple of minutes to burn off the alcohol.

Meanwhile, carefully peel the pears, removing all the skin but leaving the stalk intact. Use a small, sharp knife to remove the core in a small cone shape. Place the pears in the pan, reduce the heat, cover the pan and cook for about 20 minutes, turning the pears once half way through cooking, until cooked through. Remove the pears to a serving dish, standing them up, and leave to cool.

Remove the lavender and lemon zest from the pan and cook the liquid at a steady simmer until reduced to a quarter of the original quantity. It will be slightly syrupy. Pour the liquid over the pears, so they glisten. Serve immediately with the crème fraîche, or wait until the liquid is cold.

Plum and amaretti instant trifle

Serves 4   *15 minutes preparation: 10 minutes cooking*

I'm thrilled with this recipe. It is so simple to make and so delicious, with the added advantage that it could be adapted for as few or as many people as required. The first time I made it, I used the remains of a bottle of sweet and fizzy muscadet grape white wine to cook the plums. The next time I improvised with a glass of white wine, a little honey and sugar, but, if the plums are really ripe, you shouldn't need extra sugar, and water would do just as well as wine. Soft almond macroons are sold in a powder-blue box of 250g/8oz and are really worth searching out for their dense but light texture and intense almond flavour. A firm sponge cake, such as an all-butter Madeira cake, is an acceptable alternative. If you are making this for a dinner party, have everything ready and assemble the trifle at the last moment, either in individual bowls or one big one. And if you want to be a bit flash, dribble Amaretti liqueur over the macaroons. The ice cream isn't essential to the success of the pudding.

500g/1lb ripe plums (damsons, unless stoned after
  cooking, aren't suitable)
wine glass (about 150ml/¼ pint) white wine or water
2 tbsp sugar
1 tbsp flavourless cooking oil

50g/2oz flaked almonds
150g/5oz soft almond macaroons (*amaretti morbidi*)
  or all-butter Madeira cake
4 scoops of vanilla ice cream (optional)
200–300ml/7fl oz–½ pint Greek yoghurt

Cut the plums off their stones in big chunks. Put them in a pan with the wine or water and sugar. Cover the pan and simmer vigorously for 5–6 minutes until the pieces of plum are tender. Tip into a dish and leave to chill or pop into the freezer for about 10 minutes.

Meanwhile, heat the oil in a frying pan placed over a medium heat and when hot add the almonds. Toss constantly until lightly golden. Tip onto kitchen paper to drain.

Quarter the macaroons or cut the cake into 2.5cm/1in chunks. Place in four dishes, spoon over some of the plum juices to saturate partially, top with a scoop of ice cream, if using, then cover with yoghurt. Spoon over some of the plums, top with more yoghurt and sprinkle with the toasted almonds. Serve immediately. Yum.

Orange and vanilla poached apricots

Serves 6 *10 minutes preparation: 30 minutes cooking*

I often find myself casting around at the last moment for something to serve for pudding. Fresh fruit salad is a favourite, but dried fruit is useful too. Dried fruit used to need lengthy soaking and cooking, but these days you can buy so-called soft dried fruit which needs no soaking. A packet of these apricots, for example, is a great thing to keep in the food cupboard. I particularly like them poached in fresh orange juice and honey, and if I happen to have a vanilla pod, that goes in too. It flecks the juices with tiny black spots and enhances the flavours of this beguiling fruit. Poached like this, it could then be wrapped in puff pastry, perhaps with a slice of creamy goat's cheese, and baked until flaky and golden. I tend to do nothing more than leave the apricots to cool and serve them over a generous scoop of thick, creamy organic yoghurt. Another neat idea is to stuff each apricot with an almond. As the fruit cooks, the almonds soften and flavour the apricots from the inside. Don't forget to warn guests that the 'stone' is edible.

250g/8oz soft dried apricots
25g/1oz blanched almonds
1 tbsp runny honey

2 large oranges
1 vanilla pod
natural yoghurt to serve

Slip an almond inside each apricot in place of its absent stone. Place the fruit in a small saucepan with the honey. Use a sharp potato peeler to remove 2 x 5cm/2in strips of wafer-thin orange zest from one of the oranges. Chop it very finely and add to the pan. Place a sieve over the pan to catch the pips and squeeze over the juice from both oranges. It should just cover the apricots.

Tuck the vanilla pod down among the fruit. Place the pan over a medium heat and bring slowly to the boil, stirring a few times to melt and disperse the honey. Reduce the heat to low, partially cover the pan and simmer gently for 30 minutes. During this time the apricots will swell and absorb about half of the orange juice. Tip into a serving bowl and leave to cool.

Don't bother to remove the vanilla pod until the fruit is cold. Then it can be wiped and used again. Spoon the fruit over a mound of yoghurt to serve.

Red fruit salad with raspberry cream

Serves 2–4   *20 minutes preparation: 5 minutes cooking*

Not so long ago there was only one sort of fruit salad. It came with chunks of unpeeled apple, grapes with pips and orange with pith and skin. With the tiniest bit of care and thought, it is easy to whip up fabulous fruit salads that are easy on the eye as well as being a good balance of texture and flavour. I like making a meal of fruit salad. Sometimes I eat nothing else. This version is a particular favourite. The inclusion of a few tart redcurrants and chunks of pink or red grapefruit provides just enough sharpness to make the other sweeter fruits taste better than ever. The quantities given would be about right for four as a dessert but are envisaged as the main part of supper for two. Scotch pancakes, sold in packs of eight by all the supermarkets, are a delicious accompaniment.

250g/8oz strawberries
150g/5oz redcurrants
2 pink or red grapefuit
200g/7oz cherries
200g/7oz Flame or other seedless red grapes

2 oranges
250g/8oz Greek yoghurt
150g/5oz raspberries
icing sugar
4–8 Scotch pancakes

Place all the fruit in a suitable bowl as you prepare it. Quickly rinse the strawberries before hulling them. If the strawberries are very big, cut them into chunks. Cut medium-sized strawberries in half and leave small fruit whole. Rinse the redcurrants and pull them off the stalks.

Cut the ends off the grapefruit to reveal the pink flesh and slice the remaining skin off the fruit in big pieces. Work round the grapefruit, cutting the flesh off the 'core' in four or five pieces. Cut each piece into chunks. Cut the flesh off the cherry stones in four or five chunks. Quarter the grapes or cut in two or three slices. Halve the oranges and squeeze their juice over the fruit. Toss. Spoon the yoghurt into the middle of the salad.

Tip the raspberries into a sieve suspended over a bowl and sprinkle them with about ½ tablespoon icing sugar. Using a spoon, press the raspberries through the sieve until only the pips remain. Scrape under the sieve to collect all the pulp. Spoon the purée over the yoghurt. Pre-heat the overhead grill and lightly toast the pancakes. Dust them with icing sugar and serve with the fruit salad.

Strawberry custard fool with balsamico

Serves 6   *20 minutes preparation*

I happened on the idea of combining strawberries with balsamic vinegar by accident years ago, little realizing it had been 'invented' by, I think I'm right in saying, the Italian food writer Anna del Conte. My inspiration came from Michel Guerard's recipe for fresh fruit steeped in flavoured and concentrated red wine. It's one of several wizard desserts which have inspired me over the years from Cuisine Minceur, *Guerard's seminal gourmet dieting book. Strawberries, I discovered, work particularly well. So why not, I thought, try balsamic vinegar instead of wine? It is, after all, the must from specially cultivated varieties of grape, which is fermented, concentrated and matured in Modena, to get that special spicy, rich, peppery yet creamy and tangy flavour. It might sound odd, but if you aren't familiar with the combination I do urge you to give it a try. It is delicious alone or with Greek yoghurt. My latest variation on this theme is this fool. It went down so well when I first made it that it has become a regular which is whipped up when a luscious quick pudding is the order of the day. It is blissfully easy to make, and relies, as I often do, on ready-made fresh custard. It will keep without spoiling in the fridge for 24 hours, but it is the sort of thing to make, chill for an hour, and eat. If you do want to keep it waiting, add the toasted almonds just before you serve.*

500g/1lb strawberries
2 tsp sugar
1 tbsp balsamic vinegar

250g/8oz mascarpone
250g/8oz ready-made fresh custard
2 tbsp toasted almonds

Rinse the strawberries and remove their stalks. Set aside 6 strawberries. Quarter the bulk of the strawberries lengthways into a mixing bowl. Sprinkle with the sugar and then add the balsamic vinegar. Toss with a spoon and leave for 10 minutes, toss again and repeat if the sugar hasn't dissolved.

Meanwhile, crush the reserved whole strawberries through a sieve with the back of a spoon into a bowl. Place the mascarpone in a serving bowl or second mixing bowl. Drain the marinated strawberry juices into the mascarpone together with half the crushed strawberry juice. Beat briefly until slackened and smooth. Tip the marinated strawberries and any remaining juices into the mascarpone and amalgamate. Add the custard and loosely fold into the mascarpone.

Swirl the remaining crushed strawberry juice over the top and loosely fold in to give colour. Cover with clingfilm and chill for at least 1 hour. Scatter the almonds over the top. If preferred, transfer to individual dishes before adding the strawberry juice and almonds.

White chocolate and raspberry trifle

Serves 6 *20 minutes preparation: 5 minutes cooking, plus cooling time*

As a child I was never very keen on trifle, but as a so-called grown up I love having fun with it. I think it is very classy to simplify this childhood treat. I like to restrict the colours and flavours of the ingredients, so that the flavours and textures don't have to compete with each other. Dried apricots, for example, stewed in orange juice with vanilla, with a decoration of silver balls and dark green gelatine leaves, looks as stunning as it tastes. This trifle is classy in the extreme. White chocolate and raspberries go together almost as well as peaches and cream. They are the perfect partners in trifle.

300g/10oz raspberries
juice ½ lime
1 tbsp Kirsch, vodka or Framboise de Bourgogne
  liquer
2 tbsp icing sugar

1 Swiss roll (not chocolate)
125g/4oz white chocolate
150g/5oz double or whipping cream
2 x 500ml/17fl oz cartons fresh custard
few sprigs mint

Place 100g/3½oz of raspberries in a sieve placed over a bowl. Use the back of a spoon to push all their juice through into the bowl, leaving the pips behind. Scrape under the sieve so nothing is wasted. Add the lime juice, Kirsch, vodka or Framboise de Bourgogne and sift 1 tablespoon of icing sugar over the top. Stir well.

Slice the Swiss roll about 1cm/½in thick and use most of the slices to cover the base and make a single layer up the sides of a nice glass bowl. Moisten the slices with most of the raspberry juice and scatter with another 100g/3½oz of raspberries. Set aside 20g/¾oz of the chocolate and break the rest up into small pieces. Place the broken chocolate in a bowl and place the bowl inside another bowl filled with boiling water. Stir until the chocolate melts. This takes a few minutes, but if you want to speed it up, bring a small pan of water to the boil and suspend the bowl over the top. When it has melted, stir 1 tablespoon of the cream into the chocolate and then stir the mixture into 1 of the cartons of custard.

Pour half the chocolate custard over the prepared Swiss roll and lay the remaining slices on top. Dribble the remaining raspberry sauce over the slices and scatter with most of the remaining raspberries, reserving about 10 to decorate the top of the trifle. Use about half the second carton of custard to cover the trifle completely. Whip the rest of the cream until stiff and lift up scoops with a fork to decorate the top of the trifle.

Add the reserved raspberries. Grate the remaining chocolate on the large hole of a cheese grater over the top. Plant the mint sprigs here and there and dust the trifle with the rest of the icing sugar. Cover with clingfilm and chill for a minimum 2 hours and for up to 24 hours. Serve with the remaining custard.

Index

Acknowledgements

Many people contributed to the compilation of this book in one way or another but I particularly want to thank the staff at the 'golden triangle' of local food shops in my part of west London. They include my butcher Rodney Macken (and staff) of Macken and Bros., Dan Mortimer and staff at delicatessen, Mortimer & Bennett, Phil Diamond and his staff at Covent Garden Fishmonger, and Andrew Georghiou and staff at greengrocer C&M. Thanks too to Thai restaurant Sabai Sabai, supportive friends Andrew Payne, Helen Scott-Lidgett and Robert Osborne, my agent Bruce Hunter, son Zach John and his girlfriend Fiona Verdon-Smith for design ideas and other son Henry John, who ate most things in this book and drew the lovely illustrations. Thanks too to Joy Davies who made the food look so appetising for photography. I would particularly like to thank Bernice Davison, my original editor at the *Evening Standard*, and my mother, Jean Bareham, whose legacy paid for my lovely new kitchen, the building of which inspired this book.